A FINE LINE

NEW POETRY FROM
EASTERN AND CENTRAL EUROPE

A FINE LINE

NEW POETRY FROM
EASTERN & CENTRAL EUROPE

Edited by
Jean Boase-Beier,
Alexandra Büchler
and Fiona Sampson

with an introduction by
Fiona Sampson

PUBLICATIONS
2004

Published by Arc Publications
Nanholme Mill, Shaw Wood Road
Todmorden, Lancs OL14 6DA, UK

Design by Tony Ward
Printed by Antony Rowe Ltd.,
Eastbourne, East Sussex, UK

ISBN 1 900072 97 1

The publishers are grateful to the authors and
translators and, in the case of previously
published works, to their publishers
for allowing their poems
to be included in this anthology.

The cover illustration is
'Rocks and Seaweed (Rodel)' from
a series of nine watercolours entitled
'A Hebridean Sequence'
by Norman Adams, R.A.,
reproduced by kind permission of the painter.

The publishers acknowledge financial assistance
from Arts Council England, Yorkshire

Arc Publications Translations Series

The Publishers would particularly like to thank the following individuals and organisations for selecting, editing and co-ordinating material from the ten countries represented in the anthology, without whose participation this project would not have come to fruition:

ESTONIA
Ilvi Liive / Estonian Literature Information Centre
LATVIA
Marta Dziļuma / Latvian Literature Centre
LITHUANIA
Aušrinė Jonikaitė / Books From Lithuania
POLAND
Tomasz Pindel / Polish Book Institute
CZECH REPUBLIC
Alexandra Büchler, Literature Across Frontiers
SLOVAKIA
Stanislava Chrobáková Repar,
Editor *Romboid* magazine, Slovakia
SLOVENIA
Brane Mozetič / Centre for Slovenian Literature
HUNGARY
Anna Menyhért / JAK (Attila József Circle
Literary Union of Young Writers)
ROMANIA
Fiona Sampson, Editor *Orient Express* magazine, UK
BULGARIA
Yana Genova / Next Page Foundation

Special thanks are due to Alexandra Büchler, Director of Literature Across Frontiers, for her vision in conceiving this project and her organizational ability in setting up the network of participants.

CONTENTS

LITHUANIA

POLAND

CZECH REPUBLIC

SLOVAKIA

BULGARIA

Georgi Gospodinov

Nadezhda Radulova

Praha
14. února 2004

Antologie poezie, kterou právě držíte v ruce, je jedním z okének do duší a myslí národů, kterým bylo v nedávné historii odpíráno rozhodování o sobě samých. Ty, které vyrůstaly ve svobodných poměrech, tak mají možnost vhlédnout do nitra těch, které toto štěstí neměly a to skrze poezii, která – je-li poctivá – vymaňuje nás všechny společně z pout pomíjivosti.

*

Prague
14 January 2004

The anthology of poetry you are holding in your hands represents a window into the minds and souls of nations who have in recent history been denied the freedom to make decisions about themselves. Readers who have grown up in liberal conditions are thus given the opportunity to glimpse the inner worlds of those who were not so lucky, and to do so through poetry which – if honest – frees us all together from the bonds of ephemeral life.

Václav Havel

This anthology brings together contemporary writing by younger poets from those parts of Central and South-Eastern Europe which are identified with the European Union's project of post-Cold War enlargement. Two writers speak for each of the countries likely to have joined the EU by the end of 2007. They are writing out of a wide region of cultural territories, from the Baltic States in the north to Romania and Bulgaria in the south, whose highly differentiated countries have in common that geographical accident which placed them behind the Iron Curtain for the second half of the twentieth century.[1]

To travel across continental Europe is to be aware, of course, that national and cultural identities are not essentially bounded: not only styles of agriculture and vernacular housing but even patterns of linguistic kinship demonstrate how national boundaries are, unless policed, limitlessly porous. The transition from Tallinn to Transylvania is a gradual one, incrementally achieved; and the poets in this collection have been arranged geographically, as if on a literary Grand Tour, to reflect these transitions.

Perhaps to read a book like this is always to practise a form of cultural tourism. Certainly these poets, in their enormous diversity, do not *represent* their cultures. No two voices could sum up the complex cultural and intellectual life of an entire country: such an idea is all too redolent of the approved encounters of earlier decades. Like all poets who work *as* writers rather than for extra-textual reasons, those in this anthology represent only themselves, presenting us with a series of dazzling snapshots of contemporary poetic practices rather than a textual map of their region. They are an undeniable part of their countries' literary scenes, as are the many others not collected here: *A Fine Line*'s 'ideal reader' is that independent traveller who, excited by these examples, looks to read further on his / her own account.

To think otherwise – to read these new poetries as symptoms of particular cultural places and moments rather than as literary objects with an intentional life of their own – is to play cultural voyeur. As Václav Havel points out in his Preface, it's important for the reader of this book to situate him or herself *within* those questions of European identity which contemporary transitions pose. For Europe is not a melting pot but it is, perhaps, a soup: a *čorba* full of unexpectedly distinct – and occasionally altogether unexpected – ingredients. Sometimes this seems as cosy as a family recipe; sometimes the kitchen becomes contested territory, a stage

---

[1] Cyprus, Malta and Turkey, with their equally dramatic transitions, participate in other stories than the ones represented here.

for rival displays of power and style. In the contemporary here and now – this moment after History was Ended and then re-started, the aporia into which the twenty-first century is finding its way – the European kitchen is once again being forced to examine its traditions, sources and ways of working.

The European temperature has been raised by two contemporary pressures: one internal and one external. The internal pressure is that reflection on European identity or identities which is the result of continuing political change, both in the Balkans and as a result of the European Union's programme of enlargement. In these debates we can see the continent shift and transform from within. It is, so to speak, bubbling. The two generations of poets anthologised here, none of them over the age of forty, have broadly speaking emerged during this period of change. The oldest were scarcely more than students in 1989. But they – and we – also face external pressures, from a world which cannot stay still in the face of a new era of wars of religion. These tensions, too, seem to make themselves intimately European. There are corresponding encounters, tensions and triumphant cohabitations within Europe, from bilingual Macedonia to bilingual Wales. There is also the problem of the European legacy: complex, unparaphraseable, dangerous when it displayed imperial ambition. Faced with new sets of perceptions which subsume Europe under an imported model, the continent's multiple communities and cultures respond in a variety of ways, from disowning responsibility for these pressures to a strong – and strongly nineteenth-century – desire to spread their own cultural model as far afield as possible.

European self-identifiers vary: from common cultural heritage to particular economic scope, from human groupings to geographic coevals. But communities, even world neighbourhoods, are not categories. They're something more intrinsic; more subtle. What Europe shares is perhaps above all the *idea* of Europe, rethought by the individual and by the discursively local. A trope called 'Europe', refigured in a dozen languages, haunts this anthology. It's there in the struggle towards what Daiva Čepauskaitė satirises as 'Choice', an already-jaded consumerism – as Nadezhda Radulova, poet of stunning juxtapositions, says, "my mouth is a cheap gondola" – and the appropriation of the cultural unconscious by images from Western popular culture, as when Sergej Timofeyev resists the forces of social cohesion and readerly expectation with Mickey Mouse. By way of contrast or resistance, especially among the writers represented here from the Baltic States, is the encounter with European folk tradition, a Modernist strategy destabilised by the Estonian Asko Künnap in his encounter with a Slovenian Dream Sorcerer, in Rimvydas Stankevičius's "childish hunting of witches", in Kārlis Vērdiņš's *film noir* fairytales; as well as in the Czech writer Kateřina Rudčenková's luminous fragments which seem caught in the candle-light of dream.

For some poets this re-membering of the European place is altogether more thorough-going, even programmatic, as in Taja Kramberger's memorial to her father and to that generic paternity which is history. The tremendous sensuo-politico-symbolist energy of Emilian Galaicu-Păun's poetics throws the reader into the immediacy of encounter with his Bessarabia; for the Hungarian János Térey society and history are profoundly metaphorised, as much an internal country as a site of Real-Politik. Something similar can be seen in some of the other Central European work collected here: that of Polish poet Agnieszka Kuciak, who introduces a spiritual dialogic; of the profoundly-inventive Slovenian Primož Čučnik; and of the Slovakian Martin Solotruk, whose poetics of slippage disconcerts narrative tradition.

The poets in this book also draw a "fine line" to traditional European literary territories. There are explorations of love and relationships: Edward Pasewicz's enlarged Europe juxtaposes dreams and encounters in Prague with death in Sarajevo; Krisztina Tóth's love-letters to her life are addressed to family, friends, lovers; Petr Borkovec's ahistoric self emerges in relation to others. There are also, especially among the women represented here, explorations of individual identity. For Kristiina Ehin, writing "tenderly but without discretion", this is a deeply feminised bodily territory. Ioana Nicolaie produces a poetry of symbolic expressionism which reappropriates unexpected aspects of Romanian identity and culture. The sensibility which Katarína Kucbelová explores with fragile exactitude is part of a recognizable contemporary Slovak school, after Mila Haugová and Stanislava Repar. Finally, Georgi Gospodinov's postmodern games remind us how much of what has gone before can be situated within traditions not only of modernity and the confessional but, reaching back further, of realism and the lyric, whose nineteenth-century scale and economies of meaning – in which, faced with the unpredictable vulnerability of experience, significance is reduced to the human and the individual – remain as a marker of what might be characteristic of the European experience.

Fiona Sampson
April 2004

ESTONIA

PHOTO: TAAVI TATSI

KRISTIINA EHIN was born in 1977 in Rapla, a little town in the midst of the Estonian bogs and marshes. There, at school, she created animated cartoons and witnessed how Estonians sung themselves free from the tight embrace of the Soviet Union.

Ehin began publishing her poems whilst a student at Tartu University together with a dozen other young writers in 'The Group of Hermits' (Erakkond). Currently a graduate student, she is researching into archaic Estonian folk songs and sings in a folk music band.

Kristiina Ehin lives in Tartu and works as a translator, dance teacher and journalist. Her poetry collections include *Spring in Astrakhan* (2000), *St. Simon's Day* (2003), and *Swanbonecity* (2003).

KRISTIINA EHIN

* * *

Olen kärjekujulise universumi
suur unine emamesilane
kes magab üksi
oma taruvaikusest voodis
keset tumedat talve

tunnen selle ilmaruumi rahutuid käejooni
olen roomanud läbi iga ta musta augu

kevade tulekul
toon ilmale tuhat vastset
mu andromeedapiimast purjus
tuigerdavad nad tarust välja
et kiikuda kõiksuse avaneval õieкübaral
et veeretada valgusetolm
öötaeva tuliseks
söeks

* * *

ma olin koos õega ja ei
rääkinud sinust
kolm tundi istusime verandal
suurtes tsaariaegsetes
tugitoolides pärast äikesevihma
kardinad lehvisid
kare tekk kõditas jalgu
ja ikka veel ei rääkinud ma sinust

kui kaua võib niimoodi tummalt tunda
üksipäini mõelda maitsta ja mäletada
kas ei sarnane see üksi joomisega?

kardinad liikusid
vesipalm õitses
õrnalt ja mõõdutundetult
mu õde teab kuidas lilli kasta
ja võibolla oleks ta ka teadnud
kuidas jahutada mu
põlemasüttinud südant

* * *

I am the sleepy queen bee
of a honeycomb universe
sleeping alone
in my beehive bed
in the silence of a dark winter

I feel the restless lines in the palm of this world
I have crawled through its every black hole

spring comes
I give birth to a thousand young ones
drunk from my andromeda milk
they totter out of the hive
to swing on the opening buds of galaxies
and roll the dust of light
into the hot coal
of the night sky

* * *

I was with my sister and did not
talk about you
we sat on the veranda for three hours
in the big czarist armchairs
after a thunderstorm
the curtains wafted
and a rough blanket tickled my feet
and yet I was not talking about you

how long can I stay mute
think taste and reminisce
doesn't it resemble drinking alone?

the curtains drifted
the water chestnut blossomed
tenderly but without discretion
my sister knows how to water plants
and perhaps she would have known
how to cool my heart

aga mina ei rääkinud
kuidas me tantsisime
ja kuidas õhtuõhk õõtsutas meid
mööda õitsevaid tänavaid
ütlesin ainult
et ostsin kingad
kolme krooni eest
ja need on nii kerged
ja sametised
et hakkangi nüüd ainult nendega käima

aga ma ei rääkinud sinust

* * *

sünnitada lapsi
ürgümmargustest emakodadest
kivilinna kandilistesse korteritesse
pehme liha ja kuuma vere vahelt
valada nad betooni
liivakasti nelja nurka
mänguväljakute rõskesse rauda
lootevee loksumisest
libistada nad lifti
kärusse kile alla
auto tagaistmele
lasteaia linoleumile
oma ema ootama
ja isa igatsema

but I did not say
how we danced
and how the evening air swayed us
across blooming streets
I only said that
I bought a pair of shoes
for three crowns
and they are so light
and velvety
that now I will only wear them

but I did not talk about you

* * *

to give birth
from primeval-rounded wombs
into the angular apartments of the stone city
from soft flesh and hot blood
to pour them into concrete
into the four squares of the sandbox
into the dank iron of playgrounds
from the swish of embryonic fluid
to glide them into the elevator
into plastic prams
into the backseats of cars
on the linoleum of kindergartens
waiting for their mothers
missing their fathers

* * *

mu laps sündis ilmale mobiiltelefon käes
me ei osanud teistmoodi suhelda
olen mõistuseinimene – ei usu
südametuksete teooriasse
verekohinasse mis kõlab nagu keel
olen arukas inimene – ei usu mõtetelugemist
ega horoskoopi
mu laps sündis ilmale keemilis-bioloogilisel teel
see on teaduslikult tõestatud kuidas ta tehti!

mu laps sündis ilmale mobiiltelefon käes –
mul oli vaja ju talle teatada, et nüüd pööra pea ette
hakka sündima
lisaks korralikud keeletunnid telefoni kaudu
tahtsin et ta hakkaks kohe mõtlema,
ei raiskaks aega – kuude viisi minu ja iseenda kallist aega
silmadepilgutamise ja pöidlaimemise peale
tahtsin et ta juba väga varakult
tunneks jalgade all
karjääritee magusat maitset
ega raiskaks aega – kuude viisi minu
ja iseenda aega aga

mu laps tuli ilmale südaöösel
ja ta ei liigutanud
tal puudus miski
tal puudus see seletamatu mittemiski
mis teeb lapsest väikese karjuva puntra
ema rampväsinud süles

telefon ta tillukeste käte vahel
plinkis punast

olime ikkagi karile jooksnud

* * *

my child was born with a cellphone in its hand
we were not capable of communicating any other way
I am a woman of reason
do not believe in the theory of heartbeats
rush of blood speaking in tongues
I am an intelligent person – do not believe in either mindreading
or horoscope
my child was born chemobiologically
scientifically confirmed

my child was born with a cellphone in its hand
it rang me
and I told it to come head first
come on out
also proper language lessons over the phone
I wanted it to start thinking right away
not to waste precious time – months of mine and its own
on blinking eyes and sucking thumbs
I wanted it to feel very early
under its feet
the sweet taste of being on the career road
and not waste precious time – for months
of mine and its own but…

my child was born at midnight
and did not move
it was missing something
missing the inexplicable nothing

the phone in its little hands
was blinking red like a lighthouse

we had crashed on the rocks

* * *

kui sureme läheme surnute maale
    mõtlemata kuidas – me teame kuhu
    me näeme omaenese silmade taha
      ja südame lisajõgedesse

      pärast pikka pikka talve
      on jalatallad õrnad
     nagu nahk varsa laugudel
   kevadel kevadel – elegantselt treppidest alla
     ja siis mööda munakive
      kus veidi valus on astuda
        kingadeta

        kuum kuum päev
  kastese hommiku ja jaheda õhtu lõugade vahel
    sinu hingus närtsitab mind kuivatab mind
     põletab mu põhjamaiseid põski

   linnud jõgede kohal linnud kalmude kohal
    linnud karikakarde ja kivitreppide kohal
  linnud laidude ja latvade, linnud lagendike kohal –
        linnud linnud
       ja nende häää-ä-l

MEES JA LIND

su selja peale
on kirjutatud "mees"
loen seda et ma ei unustaks
jääpurikad tilguvad ja
koridoriuks on lahti
et saaksime nutta välja
oma naeru

kevad tuli
üle meie suleliste turjade
ja meie südamed süttisid põlema nagu
kevadkoristuslõkked

* * *

when we die we go to the land of the dead
    without thinking – we know where to go
    we see behind our eyes
       and into our hearts' tributaries

       after a long long winter
       our soles are tender as the skin on a colt's eyelids
    in the spring, in the spring elegantly down the staircases
and then along the cobblestones
       where it is a bit painful to walk

       hot hot day
between the jaws of dew-drenched morning and cool night
     your breath moistens me, dries me
       burns my nordic cheeks

    birds birds
       birds above rivers birds above graves
    birds above daises and stony staircases
    birds above isles and treetops birds above meadows
            birds birds
        and their wa-aaarble

A MAN AND A BIRD

man
is written on your back
I read it over and over to remember
icicles melt drop by drop
the hallway door is open
for us to cry out our laughter

spring storms across
our ruffled feathers
and hearts burst into flames
like the first fires of spring

need on kivid
mida mööda me hüppame
ja kumbki ei kuku
sest oskame kasutada tiibu
need on mu enda elujoonelised käed
mis segavad lindudele süüa

kui sina kaugenesid
üle ilusa porise lageda
olid linnud mulle seltsiks
sa olid müünud lapikese
oma lõpmatut merd
ja me olime rikkamad
kui kunagi enne

these are stones in the breakwater
that we jump on and off
neither of us falls
for we are skilled in using wings
these are my lifelined palms
making food for birds

when you had to go
across the shimmering wasteland
birds kept me company
you sold a patch
of your endless sea
and we were wealthier
than ever before

Translated by Richard Adang and Taavi Tatsi

PHOTO: HERKKI ERICH MERILA

Asko Künnap was born in 1971 in Tartu, Estonia, graduated from the Estonian Academy of Arts as an industrial and graphic designer and subsequently studied interior design at Oslo Art Academy in Norway. He has had two books of poems published: *In Defence of Coincidences*, a combination of his third graphic art exhibition catalogue and poetry book in 2001, and *And the Lizards Replied*, a poetry book in the form of a handbook of typography.

The art director of a Tallinn-based creative design studio and ad agency Rakett (The Rocket), he is an illustrator, designs books, board games and CD covers and runs a alternative micropublishing house, Näo Kirik (The Face Church), as well as writing poetry. He has participated in international poetry events and readings and won numerous awards for his design and art direction work. His poems have been translated into English, Finnish, Slovenian and Norwegian.

ASKO KÜNNAP

EEBENIPIMEDUSSE!

Vihmast kõlisevas kohvikus
Ljubljana kaldapealsel,
kurbade plekk-lohede taustal,
kahelpool märga lauda,
üle vaarikatee ja konjaki,
mina ja Unesnõiduja,
Vihmast pekslevas kohvikus,
suus muinasjutt ajast
kui lohede soomused
olid veel pehmed kui vein.
Ja Unesnõiduja kõneleb:
isa töötoas talveöösiti,
kui kell tolmu ja pimedust
lõikas turbaks hiirtele,
hargnes üks ristmik –
neli ust oli neljas seinas,
neli koonduvat koridori.
Sina seisid põlvini vaibas,
õhk koosnes hüüumärkidest!
Läinuks vaid otse sa,
otse edasi, silm veel kus
luuderohtu ja monsteraid
aimas aga ei seletanud.
Läinuks vaid otse, otse sa,
üksi eebenipimedusse!

Mina ja Unesnõiduja,
mantlid ikka raskemad veest,
vihmast kõlisevas kohvikus
Ljubljana kaldapealsel.

INTO THE EBONY DARKNESS!

In a café pattering with rain
on the embankment in Ljubljana,
against a backdrop of sad tin dragons,
on each side of a wet table,
above raspberry tea and cognac,
me and the Dream Sorcerer,
in the café lashing with rain,
our mouths full of the folktale
of the time when dragons' scales
were still soft as wine.
And the Dream Sorcerer speaks:
in father's workroom at night,
when the hour cut the dust and darkness
into turf for the mice,
a crossroads branched off –
the four exits in four walls,
four focused corridors.
Up to your knees in carpet,
the air was made of question marks!
If only you'd gone straight,
straight ahead, your eye still
imagining ivy and monstera
but not making them out.
If only you'd gone straight, straight ahead,
alone into the ebony darkness!

Me and the Dream Sorcerer,
coats ever heavier with water,
in the café pattering with rain
on the embankment in Ljubljana.

ALL LÕUNA-EESTI MÄGEDES

Ma sündisin tellisepurust õuele.
Ema mäletas, et sügisel.
Kuu kõndis liivakivikaljusid pidi,
Kuul minna mereni kaks laiska jõge.
All Lõuna-Eesti mägedes.

Aga nöör oli süüdatud juba,
leek kõndis kassina vastutuult.
Tolm võlvus üle teede õhtul,
moodustas maailma esimese kiriku.
All lõuna-Eesti mägedes.

Siis kohtasin naervat tütarlast,
tema juuksed olid elavast tulest.
Läbi lõhnata suve ja ateljee-ööde,
läbi ühikatubade me hoidsime käest.
All Lõuna-Eesti mägedes.

Linn linna järel langes,
Kõik tänavad voolasid mammonat.
Imeasju näidati, lennupileteid ja Lexust!
Järjest kaugemale põles nöör
all Lõuna-Eesti mägedes.

Aga orud olid endiselt alles,
veri kogunes kanjonite põhja
ja ärilõunal harjumusest ikka
käsi väitsa järgi kobas – ma olen
alt Lõuna-Eesti mägedest.

Nöör lõppes, algas püssirohi,
Telepood suleti, vihmaklõbin akendel,
savine tulvavesi voolas läbi kontorite
tuues kaasa esivanemate luid
alt Lõuna-Eesti mägedest.

Üks hakk lendab üle maastiku
mis on nüüd tardunud, ilus ja alasti,
sääsk puudutab nõiatrummi nahka
ja kummel kasvab üle varemete, tasa.
All Lõuna-Eesti mägedes

DOWN AMONG THE PEAKS OF SOUTH ESTONIA

I was born in a yard of brickdust.
Mother remembers it was autumn.
The moon wandered along the sandstone cliffs,
The moon has to take two lazy
rivers to reach the sea.
Down among the peaks of South Estonia.

But the fuse had already been lit,
the flame crawled catlike into the wind.
The dust arched above the roads of evening
forming the first church in the world.
Down among the peaks of South Estonia.

Then I met a laughing girl,
her hair was of living flame.
Through the odourless summer and studio nights,
through student rooms we held hands.
Down among the peaks of South Estonia.

Town fell after town,
All the streets flowed with Mammon.
Miracles occurred, air tickets and a real Lexus!
The fuse burned ever farther
down among the peaks of South Estonia.

But the valleys were as always,
blood collected in the depths of canyons
and at a business lunch by habit
the hand searched for the knife – I am
from down among the peaks of South Estonia.

The fuse ended, the gunpowder began,
TV shopping off the air, the patter of rain on the windows,
muddy floodwaters flowed through the offices
bringing with them the bones of forebears
from down among the peaks of South Estonia.

A jackdaw flies across the landscape
which is now congealed, beautiful and naked,
a gnat touches the skin of the witch's drum
and the camomile rises above the ruins, silently.
Down among the peaks of South Estonia.

SEE KÕIGE SUUREM NÕIDUS

See on õpetus Kõige Suuremast Nõidusest.
Kes seda valdab, selle päralt on maa ja ilm.

Kui kolmandal päeval
huntide varjud elutoa aknaisse ulatusid
(ilus sõna: Elu Tuba)
ja mahajäetud maanteed
ussidena sisisesid (ssss),
hakkasin pakkima pakke.
See juhtus Reolas –
selline raudteejaam on tõesti olemas.

Kui kolmandal päeval
tuul tõi raudteelt roostet
sealtsamast korjatud maasikatele –
piim kõik rikutud, samas nii ilus, ilus,
hakkasin pakkima pakke.
Kõigepealt varalahkund venna tuhk
ja ploomikivist tagavara silm.
(mida tähendab: Kõige Pealt?)

Kui kolmandal päeval
põlenud hekkide igemed (///X\\//)
kahelpool raudteed ütlesid:

pole suuremat nõidust kui
Mustad-märgid-valgel-nõidus,
hakkasin pakkima pakke,
et minna üle naljaka maa,
üle Tahanolla Linna, siis vee,
et saada see vana Adleri kirjutusmasin,
mille Helsingi Ülikool (seegi on olemas)
maha oli kandnud
ja tasuta ära tahtis anda.

Kolmandal päeval.

Muide, kas sa armastad mind?

THE GREATEST SPELL

These are the teachings about the Greatest Spell.
He who casts it will inherit the earth and the wind.

When on the third day
the shadows of wolves reached the living-room windows
(a beautiful word: The Living Room)
and the deserted highways
were hissing like snakes (ssss),
I began to pack my bags.
This happened in Reola –
such a station really exists.

When on the third day
the wind wafted the rust from the railway
onto the strawberries, picked on that very spot –
the milk was off, but so, so beautiful –
I began to pack my bags.
First of all, the ashes of my long-departed brother
and the spare eye made out of a plumstone,
(what does that mean: First of All?)

When on the third day
the gums of the burnt hedgerows (///X\\\V//)
on both sides of the railway said:

there is no greater spell than
The Black-Marks-On-White Spell,
I began to pack my bags,
to cross the laughable lands,
over Wannabe Town, then the waters,
to get that old Adler typewriter,
which Helsinki University (that too exists)
had written off
and was giving away for free.

On the third day.

By the way, do you love me?

KUU TANTSIB OMA TALUS

Federicole

Kuulus ülekaalus kuu,
kui sõbralikult sa lõhnad,
pealt petlikult muhe!
Kuid ma tean, Federico näitas kätte:
kuis hiid-karihiirena möirates,
kesk surnuid sa tantsid oma talus,
kaev kajamas kurja ööd.

Mu rasvakala kuu,
kui kergelt sa kõhnud!
Kõik tütarlapsed on kadedad!
Kuid ma tean, Federico kitus ära:
kuis nõiatrummi kolinal
kesk surnuid sa tantsid oma talus,
mõõk kõlkumas vennanahast vööl.

KUTSUGE ÄMBLIKUD – LAS PUNUVAD ÖÖ

Olid ööpäevad, mida ei arvutanud,
fotod, mida ei pildistanud, mäletanud.

Kutsuge ämblikud – las punuvad öö!

Ja raamatud, mida ei lugenud,
ise ei kirjutanud, ei nutnud, kaanetanud.

Kutsuge ämblikud – las punuvad öö!

Ja tüdrukud, keda ei kõnetanud,
omada ei ihanud, hiljem ei helistanud.

Kutsuge ämblikud – las punuvad öö!

Ja maamajad, mida ei ehitanud,
kolumbia kivimüür, aakritena heinamaad.

Kutsuge ämblikud – las punuvad öö!

THE MOON DANCES ON HIS FARM

For Federico

Famous overweight moon,
how friendly you smell,
so deceptively mellow!
But I know, Federico showed me:
how, roaring like a giant shrew
you dance on your farm among the dead,
the well reflecting the wicked night.

My fat fish moon,
how lightly you slim down!
All the girls are jealous!
But I know, Federico told on you:
when the drums roll
you dance on your farm among the dead,
a sword dangling from the brother-skin belt.

INVITE THE SPIDERS – LET THEM WEAVE THE NIGHT

There were days and nights uncounted,
photos untaken, unremembered.

    Invite the spiders – let them weave the night!

And books unread,
not written even, uncried for, unbound.

    Invite the spiders – let them weave the night!

And girls, remaining unaccosted,
unpossessed, later unphoned.

    Invite the spiders – let them weave the night!

And country houses, unbuilt,
Breezeblock walls, also acres of hayfields.

    Invite the spiders – let them weave the night!

Ja armastus, mida ei armastanud,
sest olid ööpäevad, mida ei arvutanud.

Kutsuge ämblikud – las punuvad öö!
Lõugkobijad, karamellist käpad
ja liiga täpne, liiga õhuline töö.

MA LOODAN LOHEDE PEALE!

Üks pärastlõuna, eksin kirikusse alleelt,
võib-olla vihmavarju, võib-olla vaikusse.
Punane tellis, koide tasane sädin,
Üks maal pimedust täis pimedal seinal.

    Häss, lohe, võts! Tule kagutuul kaenaldes!

Maali sees, pinkide naksudes rütmis,
nagu no-teatri klassikud – Lohe ja Jüri
on üksteise sisse heitluses pühendund
silm on silmas, tuhat aastat tuttavad

    Häss, lohe, võts! Söö see suvaline Jüri!

Tookord templis, kümme lennutundi siit
Draak, ma tundsin sind munkade seast,
su silmavalgeis peksles kuldne ürgaeg,
kui inimnahk üll, sa turistiparve karjatasid

    Häss, lohe, võts! Maani põleta arguse kodu!

And love, unloved,
because the days remain uncounted.

> *Invite the spiders – let them weave the night!*
> *Antenna'd jaws, paws of caramel*
> *and too exact, too aery work.*

I BELIEVE IN DRAGONS!

One afternoon, I wandered from the avenue into a church,
perhaps for shelter, perhaps for silence.
Red brick, the quiet twitter of moths,
one painting filled with darkness on the dark wall.

> *Draco, get him! Come, the south-east wind in your armpits!*

In the painting, in the rhythm of the creaking pews,
like in No theatre classics – George and the Dragon
tangled in beatified battle
eye to eye, familiar for a thousand years.

> *Draco, get him! Eat that optional George!*

Then in the temple, ten flying hours from here,
the dragon: I recognised you amongst the monks,
in the whites of your eyes ancient time thrashed,
as if wearing human skin, you were grazing flocks of tourists.

> *Draco, get him! Burn this house of cowards to the ground!*

Translated by Eric Dickens

LATVIA

PHOTO: PĒTERIS DRAGUNS

KĀRLIS VĒRDIŅŠ was born in Riga in 1979, and is studying the Theory and History of Culture at the Academy of Culture in Riga. He is a member of the editorial board of the Latvian literary magazine for young writers, *Luna*, and translates English and American poetry, notably T. S. Eliot, William Carlos Williams, Emily Dickinson and Allen Ginsberg.

His collection *Icebreakers* was published in 2001 and his *Selected Poems* in a Russian translation in 2003.

KĀRLIS VĒRDIŅŠ

PASAKA PAR ZELTA JUMPRAVU

Māte atveda mani un manus trīspadsmit brāļus un nosēdināja aiz
cirka telts. Iekšā spiedza, rūca un smējās, māte mums stāstīja:
„Tur sunīši grāmatā lasa kā mācīti vīri, sikspārņi žonglē ar paipalu
olām, un dzirdiet šos rēcienus – zvēru karalis lauva tur
pārmāca bērnus, kas gājuši gulēt ar netīrām kājām."
Te pavērās telts un pļaviņā izskrēja slaida jumprava zeltītā tērpā, uz
soliņa atkrita, ieklepojās, nopūtās grūši un mudīgi ietecēja
būdiņā raibā uz riteņiem.
Brāļi sajūsmā sāka svilpt, bet māte tos kušināja: „Klausieties, nejēgas!
Katram no jums, un arī tev, Spodri, reiz pienāks vissvētākais
brīdis dzīvē, kad sieviete ielaidīs jūs savā dārzā!
Tad nu nekavējieties daudz, bet neesiet arī dumiķi, lamzaki, atcerieties,
ko māte jums mācīja: nerunāt prasti, ar pirkstiem nerādīt,
neatstāt zābakus citiem pa kājām!"

Sāka krēslot, un bija jāiet uz mājām. Izskaitījusi bērnus, māte ar
brāļiem devās pa taciņu, es tīšām atpaliku un zagos uz būdiņu
raibo.
Pieklauvējis gāju iekšā un teicu: „Cienīgā zelta jumprava, Spodris
mans vārds, un dikti vēlos, lai ielaižat mani dārziņā savā!"
Jumpravai gulta kā siena kaudze, pušķota serpentīniem un
spīdzenītēm. Vēlīgi viņa paceļ sniegbalto roku:
„Ja vien tu apsolies nerunāt prasti, ar pirkstu nerādīt, zābakus plānvidū
neatstāt, nāc vien iekšā dārziņā manā! Daudz trušu un kamieļu
tajā ganījušies, taču sulīgas zāles pietiks i tev."
Ātri nometis zābakus, visu pasaulē aizmirsis, metos pie zelta
jumpravas siena kaudzē, lai ved nu uz dārziņu. Te atskan
baiss rēciens un milzīgs lauva izlien no bufetes, acīm lielām
kā dārzeņu plates, un neganti rēc:
„Dumjais sīpolu suska, iet uz jumpravas dārzu ar netīrām kājām!
Par to tev nokodīšu galvu kā likts, lai neapsmej manu
jumpravu!"

THE TALE OF THE GOLDEN VIRGIN

Mother brought my thirteen brothers and me behind the circus tent
and sat us down. Inside we heard shrieks, growls, and cries,
and our mother told us:

"In there, dogs are reading books like erudite gentlemen, bats are
juggling quail eggs and do you hear those cries? – the lion,
king of all animals, is teaching a lesson to those children who
have gone to bed with dirty feet."

The tent opened up and a slender virgin in a golden dress ran out
into the field, collapsed on a bench, coughed, heaved a deep
sigh, and quickly scampered into a colourful trailer on wheels.

The brothers began to whistle with excitement, but their mother
hushed them: "Listen, you fools! Each of you, and even you,
Spodris, will one day experience life's holiest moment, when
a woman lets you into her garden!

So don't delay too much, but don't be foolish, and remember what
your mother taught you: don't talk dirty, don't point, don't
leave your boots lying about!"

It began to grow dark, and we had to go home. After counting her
children, mother and my brothers headed down the path, but
I deliberately stayed behind and stole into the colourful trailer.

After knocking, I went inside and said: "Honourable golden virgin,
my name is Spodris and I would like it very much if you
would let me into your garden!"

The virgin's bed was like a haystack, decorated with streamers and
glitter. She lifted her snow-white hand:

"If you promise not to talk dirty, not to point, and not to leave your
boots lying about, you may come into my garden! Many hares
and camels have grazed there, though there are enough juicy
grasses left for you as well!"

I quickly pulled off my boots, left the world behind, and dived into
the golden virgin's haystack, so that she could lead me into
her garden. Suddenly I heard a ghastly roar and a huge lion
leapt out from under the china cabinet, with eyes as big as a
platter of vegetables, fiercely roaring:

"You stinking fool, going to the virgin's garden with dirty feet! I will
bite off your head for mocking my virgin!"

Bailēs trīcēdams skatos, kā tuvojas liesmainās krēpes. Nez kā nu
būtu gājis, ja būdiņas durvīs neparādītos māte ar žagaru rokā.
Iedzina lauvu atpakaļ bufetē, apkaunināja zelta jumpravu,
sagrāba mani aiz rokas un raudošu vilka mājās.

Paliku vēlāk par lielu vīru. Visādos dārzos mani veda, visādas
gudrības mācīja klausīt. Vēl tagad, tīrīdams lauvu būrus, dzirdu,
kā teltī šķind zelta auskari, spiedz, rūc un smejas.

KĀ BILDE

Izcel mani no plaknes, no lielās bildes smagajā zelta rāmī. Redzi –
es stāvu līdz ceļiem komposta kaudzē. Otrais no kreisās,
uzvalkā, ziedi rokā. Saspiedis lūpas, pa zodu tek smaids. Slepus
skatos – tu esi nācis pie kāda cita un paliksi vēlāk uz balli.
Prieks iepazīties, es esmu ķirbis. Bet tavas rokas šonakt pārvērtīs
mani karietē. Tā aizvedīs tevi uz klaju, dubļainu lauku, atvērs
durvis un noskatīsies, kā lietus sīkiem triepieniem cenšas tev
piezīmēt seju.

NAKTS PĀRDAUGAVĀ

Nāc, es tevi vedīšu mājās.
Tramvajs kā piedzēries kuģis noauļo pārdesmit pēdējos metrus,
pagriežas asi – lai braucēji krīt no krēsliem un pamostas –,
atvēris durvis, ielaiž vagonos tumsu.
Pēc lietus mirdz slapjie bruģakmeņi, vēlīgi vārtus ver aptieka, slimnīca,
trakomāja un kapi. Veikalu skatlogos rūķi un perfektas virtuves
iekārtas, mēs tām paiesim garām.

Shaking with fear, I watched as the fiery mane approached. Who knows what would have happened if my mother hadn't appeared in the doorway of the trailer with a switch in her hand. She chased the lion back under the china cabinet, scolded the virgin, grabbed me by the hand and dragged me home, covered with tears.

Later, I became a man. I was led into many gardens and learned to listen to wise words. Even today, while cleaning lion cages, I hear the jingle of golden earrings, shrieks, growls and cries coming from inside the circus tent.

Translated by Rihards Kalniņš

LIKE A PICTURE

Take me from that plane, from the heavy gold frame of a large picture. See – I'm standing up to the knees in a compost heap. Second from the left, in a suit, flowers in hand. Lips squeezed shut, a smile running along the chin. I look furtive – you have come with someone else and will stay later at the ball.
Nice to meet you, I'm a pumpkin. But tonight your hands will turn me into a stagecoach. It will take you to the open, dirty countryside – you'll open the door and watch how the rain tries to draw down your face in thin strokes.

NIGHT ACROSS THE DAUGAVA

Come on, I'll take you home.
The tram, charging the last ten or more meters like a drunken boat, turns sharply, – so the riders fall from their seats and wake up – and opens its doors, lets dark into the cars.
After rain the wet cobblestones shine. The drugstore, the hospital, the asylum and the cemetery open their gates warmly. In the shop windows are garden gnomes and perfect kitchen sets – we'll pass those by.

Visu nakti spuldzes blāvajā gaismā kāds sēž pie kioska, alu dzer un vēlīniem pircējiem atņem naudu. Tu viņam iedosi cigareti, un viņš mums malciņu ielies.

Mana ieliņa pēkšņi pārtrūkst milzīgas šosejas priekšā, pēdējā brīdī mēs iesprūkam kāpņu telpā. Tur balti kaķi staigā pa sienām, uz grīdas kraukšķ tukšas ampulas, koku zari attaisa logu un viegli skrubina notriepto stiklu.

Visas istabas gluži tukšas, krāsaini stari uz griestiem un sienām mums rāda kino – tur tumšā kļava aiz loga izstaipās caurā miegā, tur pagalma dobēs dīgst zāle, mans vectēvs, izmeties baltā kreklā, sēž uz grīdas un mizo ābolus.

Stari satumst, māja apstājas tumsas tuneļa vidū. Aizmiedz, tālāk tev jāiet vienam.

EŅĢELIS

"Are you my angel?"
Allen Ginsberg, *A Supermarket in California*

Jā, es esmu tavs eņģelis, šovakar izdzīts no debesīm ietīt tev celofānā gurušu vītušu āboliti, kuru tik daudzreiz vienas kāras rokas devušas otrām. Izpārdošana šonakt: zaļi augļi – ar atlaidēm, mirusi miesa – uz nomaksu.

Neteic nevienam, es esmu tavs eņģelis, Mikelandželo izdreijāts Dāvids. Ja šonakt skūpstītu manas plaukstas, dzinkstētu pirkstu kauliņu porcelāns. "Tavas debesis acu krāsā", sēktu man ausī, jo esi dzejnieks.

Nez, cik tu dabūtu, izjaucis mani un detaļās pārdevis patiltes utenī? Pudeli džina, ko viebjoties tukšot ar upeņu zapti miroņiem pilnas istabas krēslā, kopā ar svešu veci no bāra. Viņš apreibis muldēs par tankiem, promejot nozags tev naudas maku.

Šonakt aiz katras letes pa eņģelim. Vai nav tiesa, ikviens smaida platāk, nekā darba līgumā pieprasīts. Maiņa beidzas, tie, savicinājuši spārniņus, aiztrauc uz pustukšām istabiņām ar kailu spuldzi un krāsni kaktā, kur vēsās rokas saņems un nomutēs kādu mīļu un sprogainu galvu.

All night in the grimy streetlight someone sits by a kiosk, drinking
beer and taking money from late-night customers. You'll give
him a cigarette, and he'll pour us a mouthful.
My little street ends suddenly before a huge highway – at the last
second we'll dart into a stairwell. There, white cats walk
along the walls, empty ampoules crunch on the floor, tree
branches open a window and nibble lightly at the spread of
the glass.
My rooms are pretty empty, colourful beams play movies for us
on the walls and ceiling – there, in the dark, a maple
beyond the window, in the stretches of holey fog; there, in
the basement flower-beds, weeds sprout; there, my grand-
father, still in his white shirt, sits on the floor and peels
apples.
The beams blackout, the house is left in the centre of a tunnel of
dark. Sleep: you must go farther alone.

Translated by M. O. Beitiks

ANGEL

"Are you my angel?"
Allen Ginsberg, *A Supermarket in California*

Yes, I am your angel, driven out of heaven tonight to wrap a wary
wilted apple for you, an apple passed so many times from
one pair of greedy hands to another. Sale tonight: green fruit
at a discount, dead flesh by instalment.
Don't tell anyone, I am your angel, David shaped by Michelangelo;
if my hands were kissed tonight, their knuckle porcelain would
tinkle; "Your sky is the colour of eyes", ever the poet, you'd
wheeze.
I wonder how much you'd get selling my parts at the flea market?
A bottle of gin mixed with jam and drunk wincing in a dimlit
room full of dead bodies, shared with a stranger picked up at
a bar; boozy, he'd babble of tanks, upon leaving he'd snatch
your wallet.
An angel behind every counter tonight, aren't their smiles broader
than the contract requires; the shift is over, in a flutter of
wings they take off to their half-empty rooms: a naked bulb,
a stove in the corner, cool cradling hands, a kiss on that sweet,
curly-haired head.

Kungs aiz tevis jau skaita naudu. Varbūt visas plūmes un banānus, varbūt visu lieltirgotavu viņš nopirks, un mani piedevām. Noliks plauktā aiz stiklotām durvīm, bieži slaucīs ar astru slotiņu, debesis pulēs ar plīša strēmeli.
Neklaigā, neplāties. Žigli izvelc no kabatām gurķus, palūdz, lai tevi aizved uz mājām. Neskumsti, uzraksti dzejolīti.

FILMA

Šausmas pielabo meikapu un atgriežas doktora Kaligari kabinetā.
Mīļās, krāsainās Šausmas vairs nešņāks zem gultiņas draudīgas noktirnes ieplestām acīm, izstieptiem pirkstiem, un tumsa nekņudēs vēderā.
Bez skaņas slīd titri, titros upuru vārdi.

LAIKA ZIŅAS

Diktors Braiss agri no rīta rakņājas mākoņos, stumda tos uz Meksikas līča pusi un pierunā: „Cienot jūsu vēsturi un tradīcijas, mēs tomēr esam vienojušies atbalstīt patīkamāku laika apstākļu projektus".
Pilnībā kontrolē debesis. Pats tikko pamodināts, gluži silts.
Mākoņi paklausa nelabprāt – vazājas saskrāpētajās debesīs kā lieli, netīri vīrusi, kurina savstarpēju negaisu, spiežas ap diktoru Braisu.
Visas studijas sienas tiek filmētas. Tad, kad beigušās finansu ziņas, es redzu, kā sudrabains mākonis iesit Braisam, kā viņš krīt, atsizdamies perlamutra mākonī, lido, ķerdamies spalvās un gubās, līdz pazūd apakšā putekļu mākonī.
Miljoniem skatītāju visā pasaulē redz, kā vairāki melnīgsnēji mākoņi demonstratīvi nolīst. Atlikušie peld vairāku jūdžu augstumā, un sākas kultūras ziņas.

The gent behind you is busy counting his money. He'll buy all the
    plums and bananas, he'll buy the supermarket perhaps, and
    I'll be included; he'll set me on a shelf behind glass, dust me
    off with a horsehair brush, polish heaven with a strip of plush.
Stop shouting, stop bragging. Quick, take the cucumbers out of your
    pockets, request to be taken home; don't fret, write a poem.

MOVIE

Horror fixes her makeup and returns to the cabinet of Dr. Caligari.
Dear luxuriant Horror will no longer hiss under the crib, eyes wide
    in a menacing nocturne, fingers splayed; and the dark will no
    longer tingle in the pit of your belly.
Credits roll without sound, listing the names of the victims.

WEATHER FORECAST

Weatherman Brice rises early, rummages through the clouds, pushes
    them in the direction of the Gulf of Mexico cajoling: "While
    we respect your history and traditions, we still have agreed
    to lend support to projects for more agreeable weather
    patterns."
Has total control over the sky. Having just been awakened himself,
    still warm with sleep.
The clouds obey but reluctantly – they wander the scratched up
    sky like large, dirty viruses, they incite mutually assured
    thunderstorms, they crowd around Weatherman Brice.
All the walls of the studio are being filmed. Once the financial news
    is over, I see a silvery cloud take a swing at Brice, he tumbles,
    hitting a mother-of-pearl cloud, flies about and is caught in
    cirrus and cumuli, then finally disappears in a cloud of dust.
Millions of viewers around the world see how several swarthy clouds
    demonstratively pour with rain. The remaining just float
    several miles above ground, and the culture news is now on.

REMONTS

Tikai sestdienās, svētdienās un svētku dienās mēs drīkstam gulēt
vienā šķirstā – pavērt ķirmju saēstās durvis ar līku, brangu
rokturi, elpot viens otra trūdaino dvašu, visu nakti vārtīties
pīšļos.

Lai rītā, atgriežoties tur augšā, redzētu – sairusi vēl kāda pussala,
nodilis vēl kāds zemesrags, vēl daži mākoņi nokrituši uz zemes,
viss aptīts palagiem, pārklājies baltiem pelniem.

Pusdienlaikā ietrīsas zirnekļu tīkli, mēs saņemam ziņas par jaunajām
nelaimēm, kas atgadījušās visā pasaulē. Pērkam vīnu,
dodamies ciemos pie draugiem.

Pārrunājam dīvainas pašnāvības, īpaši smieklīgas bēru parašas.
Dažkārt kāds patēlo beigtu, bet citi stāsta par viņu visjaukākās
lietas un bēdā, cik ļoti tā pietrūkst.

Šai sausajā pagrabā, kur stiklos mirdz gurķi un sēnes, šūpojas sīpolu
ķēdes, un plauktos smaida oranžu ķirbju bezzobu mutes.

STATUS QUO

Atzīšanās mīlestībā – skaista kā neatkarības pasludināšana. Pēc
ilgiem opozīcijā pavadītiem gadiem ievācāmies romantiskā
dienesta dzīvoklī – pastalās, respektīvi, pliki – gadiem neizlīdām
no cisām. Un ūsainas karalienes atzina mūs *de facto*.

Šodien atkal valsts svētki un salūts, glāzītes mirdz kā ordeņi, uzkodu
vietā skūpsti. *Ergo bibamus*, mans princi, mēs nozagām veselu
valsti kā tukšu sirdi.

RENOVATION

It is only Saturdays, Sundays and holidays that we can lie in the
same casket – open the brittle door with its crooked handle,
breathe each other's stale breath, wallow in dust all night
long.
So that in the morning, returning up there, we see – another peninsula
crumbled, another cape submerged, yet another few clouds
fallen to earth, everything swaddled in sheets, covered in pale
ash.
At noon the cobwebs are aflutter, we receive news about the latest
disasters that have visited various parts of the globe. We buy
wine, go visit friends.
We discuss strange suicides, particularly funny funeral customs.
Now and then someone pretends to be dead, others tell beautiful stories and say how much he'll be missed.
In this dry cellar where pickles shine behind glass, where strings of
onions sway in the breeze and orange pumpkins grin tooth-
less on shelves.

STATUS QUO

Confession of love – beautiful like a proclamation of independence.
After many years spent in opposition, we moved into a romantic company flat – in rags, i.e., naked – and for years did
not venture outside. And moustachioed queens recognized
us *de facto*.
Today it's the national holiday again, fireworks, glasses sparkle like
medals, kisses in place of *hors d'oeuvres*. *Ergo bibamus*,
my prince, we stole an entire country like one empty heart.

Translated by Ieva Lešinska

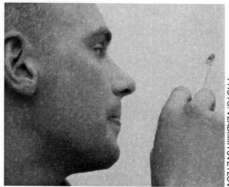

PHOTO: VLADIMIR SVETLOV

SERGEJ TIMOFEYEV was born in Riga on 13 November 1970. He studied Russian literature at the University of Latvia, and works as a freelance translator, copywriter and journalist. Since 2000, Timofeyev has been the co-ordinator of the multimedia project Orbita which involves poetry, music and video art.

He is author of three collections of poetry in Russian: *The Dog and the Scorpion* (1994), *Memoirs of a Disc-jockey* (1996), *96 / 97* (1998) and one bilingual (Russian / Latvian) book *Almost Photographs*, 2003. His poems have appeared in literary magazines in Latvia, Russia, Italy, Australia and the USA, and in anthologies, including *This Same Sky,* Four Winds Press (1993).

SERGEJ TIMOFEYEV

* * *

Приходит человек, его костюм измят.
В его лице очки на тонких дужках.
Он спорит с пустотой, он сумасшедший, ветер.
Дрожат очки на тонких дужках.
Его костюм измят, он быстро спорит.
Приходит человек и заполняет комнату.
Приходит человек, он долго шел сюда.
Его костюм измят, он спорит слишком быстро.
Дрожат его очки, он идиот, он спорит.
Он ветер, сумасшедший, он пришел.

ПИСЬМО ДРУГУ

Если бы я был моряком,
уплывал бы на полгода отсюда,
дорогой друг. А то вот
постоянно живу здесь,
хранитель, что ли.
А что хранить –
пару-другую спальных
районов, автостоянку?
Ночной кисок, в котором
небритый мужик продает
сигареты и пиво?

Впрочем, есть еще
центр с неожиданными
бюро. В которых молодые
самоуверенные люди занимаются
каким-то дизайном в хороших креслах.
А есть еще девушки, которые
запираются в туалетах клубов
и выходят с ошалевшими скрытными
лицами, переполненные горячим
золотом. Потом они превращаются
в садовые скамейки.

* * *

A man comes in, his suit is crumpled
And there are thin-rimmed glasses on his face.
He's arguing with the emptiness, he's crazy, he's a wind.
The thin-rimmed glasses quiver.
His suit is crumpled, he argues quickly.
The man comes in and fills the room.
The man comes in, he's been coming in for hours.
His suit is crumpled, he argues too quickly.
His glasses quiver, he's an idiot, he argues.
He's a wind, he's crazy, he's coming in.

Translated by Irina Osadchaja with Lyn Hejinian

LETTER TO A FRIEND

If I were a sailor
I'd sail for six months,
dear friend. But now
I live here permanently,
as a kind of keeper.
What must be maintained –
a few dormitory towns
a car park?
An all-night-store where
an unshaved old man sells
cigarettes and beer?

Beyond them a
centre with unexpected
offices. Where young self-righteous
men in cosy armchairs
create some kind of plan.
And there are girls who
lock themselves in club toilets
and come out with foggy shut
faces, full of burning
gold. Then they turn into
park benches.

Я люблю этот город,
такой же как все. Здесь
можно найти сливочные ликеры
и виртуальные игрушки
местного производства.
Есть прогрессивные
ди-джеи и есть коммерческие
ди-джеи. Есть остановки троллейбусов
с рекламой жевательной резинки.

И мы в нем тратим свои дни, как
сигареты, как бумагу для писем, как
леденцы. Задумчивые стеклодувы, мы
выдуваем лампочки с затуманенным
стеклом. Мы улыбаемся и передвигаемся,
как мишки, как мальчишки, как вспышки.
Впереди нас ведет Микки-маус, он слушает
эйсид-хаус. Но школьники готовы начать
игру. У них есть все для любви: троллейбусы
и дни рожденья. Так подожди. Телецентр
на острове, остров на реке. После ночных
программ нас всегда поджидает маршрутка.
Усатые водители помнят времена рок-н-ролла.
Пустой снежный воздух стоит высоко. Мы
отправляемся. По домам, где надо залезть
под горячий душ. По домам, где мы живем.
Где надо выспаться, позавтракать под
бормотанье новостей, сделать пару звонков.
Глоток кофе, звон ключей, мы уже далеко.
Мы стартуем в новые дни, новые серьезные
дни. И если кто-то не прав, мы расскажем ему
об этом позже. Когда все соберемся и сядем
за одним столом. Впрочем, и тогда мы будем
говорить о другом: о теннисных ракетках,
американских университетах, значении слова
"джаз". И кто-то будет танцевать, свернув ковры,
на блестящем полу. Еще раз.

I love this town,
it's like all the others. Here
you can get cream liqueur
and locally made
virtual playthings.
There are progressive
DJs and there are commercial
DJs. There are trolleybus stops
with chewing-gum ads.

And in this town we spend our days
that are like cigarettes, notepaper,
cough drops. Like thoughtful glass-blowers
we blow lamps with frosted
glass. We smile and move
like teddy bears, little rascals, flashlights.
Mickey Mouse shows us the way, listening to
acid house. The school children are ready to start
the game. They have everything needed for love: trolleybuses
and birthdays. But wait! The TV Centre
on the island, the island in the river. After the nightly broadcasts
the shabby taxi is waiting for us.
The moustached drivers remember the times of rock-'n'-roll.
The empty snowy air stands like a pillar.
We leave. Back home where we live.
Where we all have a good sleep, breakfast beneath
the murmur of the news, make a few phone-calls,
a sip of coffee, clink of keys, we are already far away.
We begin new days, new serious
days. And if any one of us is wrong we tell him
later. When we get together and sit down
around a table. But we'll also talk
about other things: tennis rackets,
American universities, the meaning of the word
'jazz'. And somebody will suddenly roll up the carpet and dance
on the shiny floor. One more time.

ОБОРОНА С МИККИ МАУСОМ

Приобрел пистолет
отстреливаюсь на девятом этаже
под моей защитой микки маус
он мой друг уже девять лун
подносит патроны по утрам
заправляемся какао
его еще немного осталось
в той большой коробке
что ты принесла с птичьего рынка
и поставила на пол
немного рассыпав

Где тебя носит
холодный упругий
ветер преступлений
микки маус читает
Робинзона Крузо сидя
на диване весь в подушках
его большие уши —
локаторы негодования
мы обязались не просить
прощения принесли клятву
на кухне глядя в зеркала
микки маус сказал
сегодня будет весело!

Заплатите за пейджер
мобильный телефон
спутниковое телевидение
пиф-паф мы дырявим газеты
но они ни при чем и микки
маус в майке с Мао
кричит в мегафон
Куда ты ушла? Возвращайся
скорей! Сегодня будет весело,
много жареной картошки
и дрянного кино о том
что все прошло как
дивизия внутренних войск

RESISTANCE WITH MICKEY MOUSE

I got myself a gun
and fought back from the ninth floor
where Mickey Mouse is under my protection.
It's been nine rising moons
since we became friends.
Every morning he brings me cartridges
we drink cocoa
there's still just a little left in the big tin
you brought from the flea market
when you put it on the floor you spilled a little.

Where are you wandering
in the cold strident wind of crimes?
Mickey Mouse is reading *Robinson Crusoe*
sitting on the couch
surrounded by pillows
his big ears –
like resistant radars.
We decided not to ask
to be forgiven,
in the kitchen while looking
in mirrors we swore,
Mickey Mouse said:
This will be a jolly day!

Pay your pager
your mobile phone
your satellite TV
piff-paff we are piercing newspapers
but it is not really their fault and Mickey
Mouse in a Mao T-shirt is howling into the megaphone:
Where did you go?
Come back soon!
This will be a jolly day –
plenty of baked potatoes and
lousy movies about
the fact that everything passed by like
a division of internal troops.

Но она не придет
ей дарят сережки с бриллиантами
и новые часы со средневековым циферблатом
где-то в Америке каждый вечер японский
ресторан они едят за столиком
в окружении верных собак
и сиреневый паж потихоньку спешит
удивительно сделать все правильно

А мы со стариной микки
перезаряжаем магазины
в обстановке хаоса и
непонимания мы образовали
Трансатлантический вал
нам не страшен Ваал
мы с горячим какао на ты
ореол доброты
вчера к нам пришел
испанский посол
долго играл на скрипке
мы ему поставили канделябр
но ему все равно было темно
отключили электричество с утра

Сегодня прислали парламентера
какую-то топ-модель
я познакомил с ней микки
они понравились друг другу
я выделил им ванную
любовь должна быть среди теней и влаги
и мохнатых полотенец
ее зовут кэнди
Королева стипендий

Постепенно образовалась степь
о ком-то там я мечтал
всегда найдется дом
чтоб посмотреть на него
но здесь было как-то приятно
без и вдруг мы встали и пошли
по ровному розовому пространству

But she's not coming
they give her presents
earrings with diamonds
a new watch with a medieval dial.
Every night somewhere in America
at the Japanese restaurant they are
having dinner at the table
surrounded by faithful dogs
and a lilac page who, astoundingly faultless,
constantly strives to do his very best.

But old Mickey and I
we created a transatlantic bulwark
in conditions of chaos and misunderstanding
we're not afraid of Baal
we are on familiar terms with cocoa,
territory of kindness.
Yesterday the Spanish ambassador came on a visit
he kept playing his violin for hours
we lighted a candelabra
but it was still too dark for him –
in the morning the electricity was shot down.

A parliament was sent here today
some super model
that I introduced to Mickey
they started approving of each other
I granted them the bathroom
love takes place amid moisture and in the shade
between furry sheets.
Her name is Candy
the scholarship queen.

Little by little the desert took shape
I was dreaming about somebody anybody
there will always be a home
to look at
but it was so nice here – without.
And suddenly we got up and walked
through evenly pink spaces

а ты там в Америке
ела лобстеров и тебе было жаль

природу?

я продам пистолет
нет расплавлю его на
газовой плите
пусть падают капли металла
я отдам микки мауса
Walt Disney & Co
(можно представить
его возражения)
ничего не осталось в пачке
какао ты вернешься может
быть в сентябре
распотрошенные лобстеры на тарелке
нас взяли.

БЕСЕДА

Красная девушка говорила синей:
«Я вчера была больной, сегодня стала
Послушной. Можете из меня
Делать пластиковые пакеты,
Можете меня отдать в посольство
Великой державы чистить что-нибудь
Ржавое. Удивительно безразличие
К собственной персоне, даже
Не хочется выйти купить новые чулки
Или китайский заводной бархат.
Хочется смотреть все время одну
Телерекламу, несложное мельтешение
Новых товаров, хочется слышать,
Как нахваливают их голоса актрис,
Чьи языки, устав от искусства счастья,
Ломаются у них во рту как льдинки.
Поверишь ли, вчера вышла из дома
И остановилась посреди двора, стояла
Так минут двадцать. В общем могла

but you in America
had lobsters for dinner and felt sorry for

nature?

I'll sell my gun
no I'll melt it on the stove
let drops of metal drip
I will give Mickey Mouse back
to Walt Disney & Co
(I can imagine his despair).
There is nothing left in the cocoa tin
maybe you will come back in September
swollen lobsters on the plate
– they finally got us.

Translated by Håkan Bravinger

CONVERSATION

The red girl said to the blue one:
"Yesterday I was sick, today I've become
Obedient. You can make plastic bags
Out of me, turn me over to the embassy
Of the great country to clean something
Rusty. I've an amazing indifference
Towards my own person, to the point
Where I've no desire to go out and buy new stockings
Or Chinese industrial velvet.
All I want to do is watch the same
TV commercial over and over, to watch simple images
Of new products, hear
The voices of actresses praise them,
Their tongues, exhausted from the art of happiness
Cracking in their mouths like ice cubes.
Can you imagine, I left the house yesterday
And stopped in the middle of the courtyard, stood there
Like that no less than twenty minutes. I could, in fact, have
Taken off for outer space like

Бы и улететь в космос, как собачка
Безропотная. То ли жизнь моя из меня
Уходит, то ли это новая эра, даже
Плюшевые игрушки мне не милы.»
Говорила синяя девушка красной:
«Все верно, все очень похоже,
В супермаркетах как на Луне,
И я гуляю, длинными ногтями
Касаясь краешков огромных коробок.
Это болезнь поражает девушек
И только, мужчины от нее
Лечатся боксом, табаком, водкой,
А то бы и они треснули по швам,
Вывернулись бы наизнанку, оглохли.»
Сидели две девушки и говорили,
Всегда спокойно, всегда о важном,
А вокруг стояли сонные вещи,
Уставшие столики, пьяные кресла.
Это было в одной большой квартире,
Чьи окна выходят на улицу в центре,
В центре города, города у моря,
Серого моря, зеленой воды.

A compliant doggie. Either life is leaving
Me, or a new era is beginning, not even
Stuffed animals do it for me any more."
Then the blue girl said to the red one:
"Right you are, everything's so alike
Both in supermarkets and on the moon,
And I walk around, touching the sides
Of large cartons with my long fingernails.
This illness is common only
Among girls, men cure themselves
With boxing, tobacco and vodka,
Otherwise they'd come apart at the seams,
Turn inside out, go deaf."
So the two girls sat and talked,
Always quietly, always about what's important,
And around them objects slumbered:
Exhausted tables, drunken chairs.
It all took place in a large apartment,
Overlooking a downtown street,
The downtown of a city, a city by the sea,
The sea of grey, the water of green.

Translated by Ieva Lešinska

LITHUANIA

PHOTO: ROMUALDAS RAKAUSKAS

Daiva Čepauskaitė was born 1967 in Marijampolė, took acting classes at the Kaunas Youth Musical Studio and graduated from the Kaunas Medical Academy as a physician. A poet and a dramatist, she is a member of the Lithuanian Theatre Association and the Lithuanian Writers' Union. Since 1990, she has been employed full-time as an actress by the Kaunas Youth Chamber Theatre.

She has published two collections of verse and is also known as an author of plays for children, a number of which have been staged by the Kaunas Youth Chamber Theatre and the Kaunas Puppet Theatre.

DAIVA ČEPAUSKAITĖ

POEZIJA

Esu karvė, vardu Poezija,
duodu šiek tiek pieno,
paprastai 2,5% riebumo,
kartais pavyksta
išspausti ir iki trijų,
didžiuojuos, kad jis apdirbamas
pažangiausia technologija
ir popieriniuose tetrapakuose
pasiekia nereiklius vartotojus,
sergu visomis ligomis,
kurios nesvetimos gyvai būtybei
ir kruopščiai aprašytos
veterinarijos vadovėliuose,
ganausi geroje bandoje
(kolektyvas draugiškas,
kalbos barjerų nėra),
bijau sparvų ir zootechniko,
galiu būti ir kitaip naudinga –
užėjus šalnoms, kai nusilengvinsiu,
įlipk į mano krūvą basas,
pamatysi – tokia šiluma,
nuo padų pakils
iki pat pakaušio.

PASIRINKIMAS

> *Renkuosi įsidėt į galvą net tą galimybę, kad*
> *gyvenimas turi savo logiką.*
> Wisława Szymborska

Išsirinkau gimimo dieną
  banaliausiu metų laiku,
  mėnesį, panašų į šlapią
  karvelio jauniklį,
  lūžusiu raktikauliu.

Išsirinkau vietą smėlio dėžėje,
  troleibuse, lovoje, prie stalo,
  laikraščių puslapiuose, akyse, liežuviuose,
  visų aptvare ir niekieno kaimynystėje.

POETRY

I am a cow named Poetry,
I give a little milk,
usually 2.5% fat,
sometimes I manage
to squeeze out 3%,
I'm proud that it's processed
with the most advanced technology
and in paper tetrapacks
reaches undemanding users,
I am sick with all the diseases
not unknown to living things
and carefully detailed
in veterinary textbooks,
I graze in a good herd
(the collective is friendly,
there are no language barriers),
I am afraid of horseflies and the zoo technician,
I can be useful in other ways too –
when the cold comes, when I defecate,
climb into my pile barefoot,
you'll see how the warmth
rises from your feet
up to the back of your head.

CHOICE

> *I am preparing to put inside my head even the*
> *possibility that life has its own logic.*
> Wisława Szymborska

I chose a birthday
in the most banal season of the year,
  a month much like a pigeon's
  wet chick
  with a broken collarbone.

I chose a place in the sand box
  on the trolley, in bed, at the table,
  on newspaper pages, in the eyes, on tongues,
  in everyone's enclosure and no one's neighbourhood.

Išsirinkau vaizdą pro langą –
  kvadratinį natiurmortą su girtuokliu,
  velkančiu šunį (maniau, skarmalą).

Išsirinkau suknelę – šiandien išeiginė,

išsirinkau bandelę su aguonomis,

išsirinkau mylimą – ne tą,
  apie kurį pagalvojot,

išsirinkau Velykas ir Kalėdas
  ir abiem po žadintuvą,
  kad nepramiegočiau,

išsirinkau kūno temperatūrą,
  nagų ilgį ir dantų formulę,

išsirinkau kančią 6val per parą,
  6% laimės ir kiaulienos karbonadą,

išsirinkau sparnus, uodegą,
  žvynus, kanopas, iltis,
  darbo įrankius ir dauginimosi būdą,

išsirinkau himną, herbą,
  filosofinį pamatą ir nepateisinamas priežastis,

išsirinkau tikėjimą, didžiąsias nuodėmes,
  reikalingus parašus bei rekomendacijas,

išsirinkau mirtį – ne lietui lyjant,
  ne ketvirtadienį, ne ant laiptų pas mylimą,
  iš kuklumo.

I chose a view out of the window –
  a square still-life with drunk
  dragging a dog (I thought a rag).

I chose a dress – today a holiday,

I chose a loaf with poppy seeds,

I chose a lover – not the one
  you thought of,

I chose Easter and Christmas
  and an alarm clock for each
  so I would not oversleep,

I chose my body temperature
  the length of my nails and shape of my teeth,

I chose suffering 6 hours per day
  6% happiness and a pork chop,

I chose wings, tail,
  scales, hooves, fangs,
  work tools and method of reproduction,

I chose a national anthem, coat of arms,
  philosophical foundation and unjustifiable causes,

I chose a faith, mortal sins,
  necessary signatures and recommendations,

I chose death – not when the rain is falling,
  not on a Thursday, not on the stairs at my lover's,
  out of modesty.

* * *

Dar apeisiu gyvulius,
žieminių svogūnų lysvę,
apvalų galukiemio akmenį
ir storiausios kaimynės užpakalį,
dar aplankysiu tą mažą senutę,
patyliukais nuvalgysiu uogienę,
kad pagalvotų – rupūžės, vagys,
dar pasikasysiu kuprą
į pernai nušalusį lazdyną,
iškrapštysiu iš obuolio kirminą
ir paleisiu į laisvę,
paskui pasižiūrėsiu pro rakto skylutę,
kaip nekenčia tie, kurie myli,
tada nuvarysiu pirmą pasitaikiusį
dviratį su skambučiu,
važinėsiu per naktį
ir kelsiu tokį triukšmą,
kaip pats garsiausias kompozitorius,
paskui padėsiu galvą
už tėvynę ir švelniausią merginą,
tada susirasiu patį
linksmiausią žmogų,
patapšnosiu per petį ir pasakysiu –
dabar tu.

LOPŠINĖ MYLIMAJAM

Durneli, tu mano,
durneli,
vienu du gyvi telikome,
visi seniai mirę,
nuprausti, nuskusti,
sušukuoti, nugrimuoti,
apraudoti, palaidoti,
tvarkingai išrikiuoti,
gėlėmis apkaišyti,
ilsisi ramybėje
be jokios rizikos.
Vienu du niekaip
negalime numirti,

* * *

I'll make my round of the animals,
the furrow of winter onions,
the oval stone at the yard's edge
and the fattest woman neighbour's behind,
I'll visit that little old woman,
stealthily eat all the preserves,
so she thinks – bastards, thieves,
I'll scratch my back
against the nut tree that froze last year,
dig the worm out of the apple
and set it free,
then I'll watch through the keyhole
how those who love hate,
then I'll steal the first bicycle
I find with a bell,
I'll ride around all night
and will raise such a ruckus
like the most famous composer,
then I'll lay down my head
for my country and the gentlest girl,
then I'll find
the happiest person,
will tap him on the shoulder and say –
now you.

LULLABY FOR A LOVED ONE

You fool, my little
fool,
only the two of us are left,
everyone else is long dead,
washed, shaved,
combed, made up,
mourned, buried,
neatly lined up,
decorated with flowers,
resting in peace
with no risk.
We alone can find
no way to die,

krentame žemyn galva
vis į tą patį dangų,
vis iki kito karto.
Akių kampučiuose
budi dvi kanarėlės,
skirtingos kaip dvi
vieno žmogaus akys,
durneli, tu mano,
durneli,
šiąnakt ir vėl niekaip
negalime numirti,
šiąnakt verkiu kanarėlėmis,
ir mano ašaros čiulba.

* * *

Kaip gyveni?

– Gerai, sakau, gerai.
Išsimiegojau.
Nieko nesapnavau.
Atsikėliau savo noru.
Pažiūrėjau į veidrodį.
Nepamačiau nieko neįprasto.
Prisiminiau vieną kitą žmogų.
Vieno kito neprisiminiau.
Nuvaliau trupinius nuo stalo.
Radau raziną.
Atidariau langą.
Kartą jaučiausi laiminga.
Du kartus nelaiminga.
Tris kartus niekaip nesijaučiau.
Kartą pagalvojau apie gyvenimo prasmę.
Du kartus apie beprasmybę.
Tris kartus nieko negalvojau.
Kosėjau.
Nieko neskaudėjo.
Nieko netrūko.
Niekam nerūpėjau.
Žiūrėjau žinias.

fall head first
always into that same sky,
always until the next time.
In the corners of our eyes
stand two canaries,
different as two
of the same person's eyes,
you fool, my little
fool,
tonight once again we can find
no ways to die,
tonight I weep canaries
and my tears sing.

* * *

How are you doing?

– Fine, I say, fine.
I slept well.
Dreamed nothing.
Woke up on my own.
Looked into the mirror.
Saw nothing unusual.
Remembered one or two people.
One or two I didn't remember.
Wiped the crumbs off the table.
Found a raisin.
Opened a window.
Felt happy once.
Unhappy twice.
Didn't feel anything three times.
Thought about the meaning of life once.
About meaninglessness twice.
Thought about nothing three times.
Coughed.
Nothing hurt.
Nothing was lacking.
No one worried about me.
Watched the news.

Perkirpo juostelę.
Davė interviu.
Bombardavo.
Nuskendo du vaikai ir automobilis
(atskirai).
Apie automobilį pasakojo ilgiau
nei apie vaikus.
Dirstelėjau į kiemą.
Dirstelėjau į piniginę.
Žvilgtelėjau į praeitį.
Sudėliojau praradimus.
Pasidžiaugiau atradimais.
Apžvelgiau įvykius.
Apmąsčiau kontekstą.
Įvertinau objektą.
Suradau sąsajas.
Išsiaiškinau priežastis.
Pagerbiau tylos minute mirusius.
Atsidusau dėl mylimo.
Pagalvojau apie motiną.
Persirengiau.
Pasikasiau pakaušį.
Gerai, sakau, gerai.

They cut the tape.
Gave an interview.
Bombed.
Two children and a car drowned
(separately).
They talked about the car longer
Than about the children.
Glanced into the yard.
Glanced into my wallet.
Looked into the past.
Laid out my losses.
Rejoiced in my discoveries.
Surveyed events.
Contemplated the context.
Evaluated the object.
Discovered connections.
Explained the reasons.
Honoured the dead with a minute of silence.
Sighed because of my lover.
Thought about my mother.
Changed my clothes.
Scratched my head.
Fine, I say, fine.

Translated by Jonas Zdanys

PHOTO: ALGIMANTAS ŽIŽIŪNAS

RIMVYDAS STANKEVIČIUS was born in 1973 in Elektrėnai and graduated from the Philology Faculty of Vilnius University with a master's degree in Lithuanian literature. Since 1997 he has worked for the *Respublika* daily as a news reporter and in 2001 he hosted the TV show 'A Cultural Trap'.

He made his debut as a poet in the annual poetry anthology *Spring of Poetry* in 1993 and his verse has subsequently been published in literary magazines, anthologies and newspapers. His first collection of poetry, *An Eye*, was published in 1996.

Stankevičius' poetry has been translated into Polish, Swedish, Finnish, and English and has appeared in numerous anthologies abroad. He has also written lyrics for over twenty rock songs and in 2002, with the composer Rokas Radzevičius, he produced a rock opera *Jūratė and Kastytis*. At present, he lives in Vilnius.

RIMVYDAS STANKEVIČIUS

KARTA

Vaikiška raganų medžioklė.
Kaip ir kasnakt stovim visi
po kvarco dušu – pusnuogiai, jauni,
beveik patenkinti,
dar garuojantys sapnų likučiais:
tie, kur prabudę iš karo, rūgščiai kvepia žeme;
gėdijas rankų virpėjimo tie, kur iš meilės sūpynių;
suglebę ir skaidrūs – ragavę mirties…
Pažinti galima, bet kuo gi apkaltinsi,
Kai laikmečio pirštas vis rodo
Į vėliavas –
Vėliavos baltos
Kartoja: nekaltas, nekaltas…

KARTĄ PER METUS. VIEŠKELIS

Žinau ko ateini mama
tam ir yra
nerakintos durys pernakt
negesinta šviesa kišanti
šiurkštų snukį
artyn

Tam ir yra šitas vieškelis
kuriuo tiktai tu
kuriuo tiktai eitum ir eitum
net prieš gaidgystę kai šerkšnas
stvarsto už
kojų

Žinau tai tavo samdyti
elegantiški skausmo
pirštai sutvarkantys patalą
užsagstantys marškinius
po to jau palangėn
barbenantys

GENERATION

Childish hunting of witches.
As every night we all stand
under a shower of quartz – half naked, young,
almost satisfied,
still steaming with the remains of dreams:
those woken from war smell of sour earth;
those from the swing of love have the flush of trembling hands;
limp and limpid – those who tasted death...
You can recognise them, but of what to accuse them,
when the finger of time points constantly
to standards –
white standards
repeat: not guilty, not guilty...

ONCE A YEAR. A COUNTRY ROAD

I know what you are coming for Mum
that's why
the door's unlocked all night
the light's not out it pokes
its coarse snout
closer

That's why there's a country road
along which only you
along which only you'd walk and walk
even before cockcrow when hoarfrost
grabs the legs

I know it's your hired
elegant aching fingers
making the bed
buttoning the shirt
later on tapping
on the windowsill

Laukiu ir aš
imsim patręšim
žodžiais ramybę

– Kodėl, vaikeli, kodėl?
Kas gi tau šovė į galvą?

– Aš pats, mama.

TYLINČIŲJŲ YRA KARALYSTĖ

Šimtmečius tyli sustingę miestai

Amžinas meilės judesys
Žvilgsnis pro langą
Amžinas žingsnis per slenkstį
Žodis kyšantis iš pusiau pravirų lūpų

Amžinas išdidumas ir skurdas
Lietus pakibęs virš ištroškusios žemės
Ir amžinai tas pats kiemsargis
Kas rytą tingiai slampioja
Su šluota rankoje

Bet jis iš kitos karalystės

DINGUSIŲJŲ YRA KARALYSTĖ

Jie nieko nežino
Sako kaip ir per amžius
Tingiai dūzgia saulė ir
Margaspalviai paukščiai kyla
Krūtinėmis taškydami spindulius
Net neprisimena
Ar būtų matę ką nors ar bent šešėlį jutę
Švari sako žemė sapnai ir giesmės

I'm also waiting
finally we will top-dress
the silence with words

– Why, sonny, why?
What got into your head?

– I'll manage myself, Mum.

THE KINGDOM BELONGS TO THE SILENT

Petrified cities are silent for ages

The eternal movement of love
A glimpse through a window
The eternal step over the threshold
A word sticking out of half-opened lips

Eternal pride and poverty
Rain hanging over the thirsty earth
And every morning the same sweeper
Loiters around idly
With a broom in his hand

But he's from another kingdom

THE KINGDOM BELONGS TO THE LOST

They don't know anything
They say the world is without end
The sun hums lazily and
Mottled birds take wing
Splashing sunbeams with their breasts
Not even remembering
If they saw anything or felt at least a shadow
They say the earth and dreams and chants are pure

Ir romūs žvilgsniai nuslysta per dangų
Kyla prie lūpų pirštai
Ir spaudžias arčiau vienas kito į krūvą visi
Trys gyvieji ir tuzinas mirusiųjų

NEKANONIZUOTAS

Tuščia ir gili
Yra karalystė
Šalta sunki
Tolydžio mažėjanti
Ankšta ir vimdanti
Yra karalystė
Noris sakyt kad
Niekieno – –
– – – –
– –

Mūsų

APOLOGY

Žvaigždes juodai užtapiau
Atleisk
Negalėjau užmigti
Eiti ir klupti ir eiti tavęs pasitikti
Ten kur toli kur skaudžiau ir tikriau
Aš nepabūgau aš tik nutilau arba tarkim miriau
Ir patikėk netgi šitai net šitai galėtų turėtų užsnigti

Meek glances glide over the sky
Fingers mount to lips
They all huddle closer to each other
Three living and a dozen dead

UNCANONISED

Empty and deep
The kingdom
Cold heavy
Continually diminishing
Cramped and emetic
The kingdom
One wants to say
Nobody's – –
– – – –
– –
Ours

APOLOGY

I painted the stars in black
Sorry
I could'nt fall asleep
Go to stumble and go to meet you
There far away where it's more painful, more honest
I didn't get scared I simply became silent
Or let's say died, and believe me
Even this even this might be snowed in

DIMINUENDO

kodėl taip žemai
kabini virš manęs
suplėšytą sielvarto veidą
naktie

turiu maldų
sunkesnių už tave
turiu žodžių
galinčių perrėkti
tavo buvimą

priešmirtinį žuvies
pliaukšėjimą
laikrodžio lūpose

keturias
raudų sienas
ir tik vieną prašymą

palauk kol užmigsiu

DIMINUENDO

why hang
this torn face of sorrow
so low over me
at night

I have prayers
heavier than you
I have words
able to drown out
your very being

I have the flop
of a fish before death
in the lips of a clock

four
wailing walls
and only one request

please wait until I fall asleep

Translated by Eugenijus Ališanka
and Kerry Shawn Keys

POLAND

PHOTO: KAROLINA SIKORSKA

AGNIESZKA KUCIAK lives in Poznań and lectures on Polish literature of the Romantic era and the works of Dante. She is known for her translations from the Italian and has published a new edition of Dante's *Inferno* and a collection of sonnets by Petrach.

Her first collection of poems, *Retardation* (2001), is considered the most outstanding Polish poetry first collection of the past decade. Characterised by wit, irony and humour reminiscent of Wisława Szymborska's work, it represents the 'Polish school of poetry' in its concern with existential issues and human experience.

AGNIESZKA KUCIAK

METRUM

Czasem to jest jak powrót. Już przed progiem
psy ogonami rozgarniają lata
nieobecności. Można znów pogłaskać
ich kudły, stary stół, pryszczatość drogiej
ściany z podziałką – mapy dat i imion,
z którą mierzyło się w dzieciństwie, pragnąc
wciąż wyżej wrastać w nią wraz z każdą linią.
Tak jak się mierzy z metrum: stając wobec
muru papieru, dat i imion, wiary
w ścianę, do której zawsze można podbiec
z gorzkiego deszczu znów pod rynnę rymu.
A czasem jest jak los, co lubi zamknąć
zamiar cezurą lub przerzucić w inny
wiersz, gdzie już nie ma domu i rodziny.

* * *

Do każdej rzeczy długo puka deszcz
i pyta: "Jesteś?" A ja mówię: "Nie,
wcale mnie nie ma." Deszcz jest mistrzem zen.
Może wylanym z nieba za klaskanie
zbyt przezroczystą jedną dłonią?
                                        Siądź,
(*Bo kto ogrodu swego nie uprawia,
tego zarasta dziki, dziki bóg*),
darmowej lekcji słuchaj, nadaremnie
powtarzaj za nim małe, ciche "tak",
które cię zniszczy.

(Kropla po kropli, jak w ten wielki wieczór,
kiedy przekupień chciał nam sprzedać róże,
lecz nie chcieliśmy żadnych róż, chcieliśmy
całego życia.)

METRE

Sometimes it's like coming home. Before you cross the threshold
the dogs are already brushing aside the years of absence
with their tails. You can stroke their shaggy
old table-top again, the pimply surface of the dear
calibrated wall – a map of dates and names
you were measured by in childhood, longing
to keep on growing higher into it with every line.
That's how you measure with a metre: standing against
a solid bulwark of paper, dates and names, and faith
in the wall you can always run up to
out of the bitter rain, back beneath the gutter of rhyme.
And sometimes it's like fate wanting to cut off
your intention with a caesura or cast it into another
poem, where there's no more home or family.

* * *

For ages the rain keeps knocking at each thing
and asking: "Are you there?" But I say: "No,
I'm not here at all." The rain is a Zen master.
Maybe it was poured out of heaven for clapping
with a single, too-transparent hand?
                            Sit down,
(*For he who fails to tend his garden*
will be overgrown by a wild, wild god),
listen to a free lecture, and pointlessly
repeat after it a quiet little "yes"
that will destroy you.

(Drop by drop, like on that great evening
when the peddler wanted to sell us roses,
but we didn't want any roses, we wanted
the whole of life.)

WAGARY W ŚWIĘTO

Że w najlepszego nawet Pana Boga
wstępują diabli – każde dziecko wie.
Więc w uciekaniu przed nim nad jezioro
więcej niż racji było strachu. Nawet
pływając, jeszcze składaliśmy dłonie
i długi pokłon. Smak na podniebieniu
      –   nieba? obłoków sądu? połkniętego
wodnego lustra? – miał pozostać gorzki.
Pozornie lekko musowała w wodzie
– jak rozpuszczalna oranżada – nasza
nieletnia dusza. Rozpuszczone dzieci!
Zasłużyliśmy na porządne lanie:
apokalipsę, gorejący krzew.

W DOMU DUSZY

Mam urojenie, że żyję, i zdrowy chodzę po świecie,
a tak naprawdę leżę w domu duszy.
Wciąż ukazują mi się tutaj ludzie,
a nie anioły. Mówią językiem człowieczym
słowa: "Dzień dobry, co u pana słychać?"
A ja: "Dziękuję" – mówię – "Słychać głosy."
Co dzień oglądam, nie w światłości, w świetle
dnia albo zmierzchu, kształty i kolory;
pomiędzy Bogiem a Szatanem wszystkie
święte odcienie, a ich samych nie.
Dotykam twarzy jej tak delikatnie,
jak gdyby Kain nie mógł zabić Abla,
szczęśliwy bez jego ekstaz.
Mam takie banalne omamy (woń trawy i świergot jaskółek),
że pan doktor słucha mnie znudzony.
Nagle otwiera otchłań swoich ust,
a potem mówi mi, że te objawy
wkrótce ustąpią, że mi nic nie będzie.
Zapewnia: "nie będzie Nic".

PLAYING TRUANT ON SUNDAY

The devil can get into the very best of us,
even the Lord himself, as every child knows.
So in running away from him to the lake
our motive was fear more than reason. Even
while swimming we still had our hands folded
and our heads bowed low. The taste on our palates
– of heaven? the clouds of judgment? a gulp
of the water level? – would remain bitter.
Our under-age souls seemed to fizz
in the water gently – like dissoluble
orangeade. What dissolute children we were!
We deserved a good, sound thrashing:
an apocalypse, or a burning bush.

IN THE HOUSE OF THE SOUL

In my fantasies I'm alive and well, going about the world,
but in actual fact I'm lying in the house of the soul.
It's people that keep appearing to me here
and not angels. Talking in human language they say
the words: "Good day, how are things?"
And I say: "Fine, thank you, I'm seeing things."
Every day I take a look, not in brilliance, in the light
of day or dusk, at shapes and colours;
at all the sacred shades in between
God and Satan, but not at either of them.
I touch her face as gently
as if Cain could not have murdered Abel,
blissful without his ecstasies.
I have such banal delusions (the smell of grass and the twitter of swallows)
that the doctor gets bored listening to me.
Suddenly he opens the chasm of his mouth,
and tells me that these symptoms
will vanish soon, and then I'll have nothing.
"You'll have Nothing", he assures me.

KOŚCIÓŁ

Tak dziwnie tam się objawia nasza ciałożerność:
przyjmujemy doustnie, tak jak chorzy lub dzieci,
kęs Tajemnicy. To, co połykamy,
ma papierowy smak białego wiersza
i taje w ustach jak święcony śnieg.

I taka dziwna tam nasza niedzielność,
gdy spowiadamy się nie z samotności
czy cudzej winy. I wdychamy zapach
Ducha świętego: miłość i kadzidło.
Jest światłem naszych zezowatych serc.

Inne prócz takich cuda się nie dzieją,
nie dostajemy żadnych świętych mejli,
P.B. nie dzwoni, nawet na oddziale,
oczekujący wciąż na przeszczep duszy,
widzą w swych wizjach ekstatycznych tylko
psychotropowy opłatek.

* * *

Przez roztargnienie rzucić pomarańcze
do tego grobu – jakież to *"fałks pałks"*!
Przez małą chwilę w duszy poznanianki
toczy się walka: czy dla siatki słońc
(tym droższych sercu, że kupionych tanio,
tym słodszych jeszcze, że być miały z pieprzem)
zejść jak Orfeusz, jak Eneasz, Dante
między pomarłych? I z pomarańczami,
nie z nim, powrócić do zgorszonych lekko
tym żałobników?
                    I decyzja: zostać
i do wielkiego dodać mały żal.

THE CHURCH

How strangely our flesh-eating manifests itself there:
just like sick people or children we orally ingest
a morsel of the Mystery. The thing we swallow
has the papery taste of a verse with no rhyme
and melts in the mouth like consecrated snow.

And how strange our weekend mood there is,
as we make our confessions not out of loneliness
or someone else's fault. And we breathe in the smell
of the Holy Ghost: love and incense.
He is the light of our cross-eyed hearts.

Besides these, other miracles just don't happen,
we don't get any holy e-mails,
The L. G. doesn't call, not even on the ward,
and those who keep on waiting for a soul transplant
see nothing in their ecstatic visions
but a psychotropic wafer.

* * *

Absent-mindedly dropping oranges
into the grave – what a "*fauks pauks*"!
For a short while in the Poznań woman's soul
a battle rages: should she, for a net full of suns
(all the dearer for being bought cheap,
and so much sweeter you could have them with pepper),
descend like Orpheus, like Aeneas or Dante
among the dead? And not with him, but with the oranges,
return to the slightly scandalised
mourners?
        And the decision: she'll stay put,
and to the very great pity add a small one.

Translated by Antonia Lloyd-Jones

PHOTO: ARTUTR BURSZTA / BIURO LITERACKIE

EDWARD PASEWICZ, a poet and literary critic, was born in 1971 and lives in Poznań. His first full-length poetry collection, entitled *Lower Wilda*, which appeared in 2002 to critical acclaim, introduces openly gay themes into young Polish literature.

EDWARD PASEWICZ

EGZOTYCZNEJ RYBIE Z AKWARIUM W CAFE 2000

Gdybym mógł przełożyłbym cię z obcego
albo napisał od początku we własnym języku.
Za grubą szybą ty i ja mamy przyciężkawe
sylwetki
wyciętych z kartonu kukiełek.

Ja pracuję bardzo nad sposobem widzenia,
podglądam świat przy sąsiednich stolikach –
przystojnego studenta i Wojaka-brzuchacza i
dwóch lesbijek z których jedną znam
od dziecka – ty podglądasz nas.

Jesteś grubą szarą kiełbaską z wyłupiastymi
oczami,
co chwila przylepiasz się do szyby
otworem gębowym i zsuwasz się w dół.
Właściwie nic ważniejszego ponad to.

Chociaż to obce, obce, obce.

Nijak się tego nie da oddać tutaj.
Wojak-brzuchacz już za chwilę zaśnie
i będzie ginął pod Sarajewem, rażony
sztucznym choinkowym ogniem,
Student wymieni spojrzenia z Barmanem i
dwie lesbijki, z których jedną znam
zasną wtulone w siebie na kanapie.

NAUKI DLA ŻEBRAKÓW NO. 3

W "Brass Rail" (Minneapolis)
siedzę sobie, nowoczesny Faust.
Refleksy dają po oczach i czuję
się jak zdeptana stokrotka. Do
resztek w szkle wydymam wargi
i myślę, jak by było, gdyby w wargę

TO AN EXOTIC FISH IN THE AQUARIUM AT CAFÉ 2000

If I could I would translate you from the alien
or write you from scratch in my own language.
Behind thick glass you and I both have
the overheavy silhouettes
of marionettes cut out of cardboard.

I'm working hard at a way of seeing,
watching the world of the neighbouring tables –
a handsome student, a beerbellied recruit, and
two lesbians, one of whom I've known since
childhood – you're watching us.

You're a thick, grey sausage with bugged-out eyes,
every now and then you fasten your orifice
to the glass and slide down to the bottom.
It's really nothing more than that.

But it's alien, alien, alien.

And there's no way to render it here.
In a moment, Private Beerbelly will pass out
and fall outside Sarajevo, stricken
with a fusillade of New Year's firecrackers.
The student will exchange glances with the bartender,
and the two lesbians, one of whom I know,
will fall asleep in each other's arms on the sofa.

LESSON FOR BEGGARS NO. 3

In the "Brass Rail" (Minneapolis)
I just sit there, a modern Faust.
Reflected light trips up my eyes and I feel
like a trampled daisy. I pucker my lips
for what's left of my drink
and imagine my lips

ukąsił mnie skorpion albo inna
gadzina. Łuski na ciele, przemiana,
czy powolne zdychanie ze
zniekształconą twarzą. Alkohol
odkaża, odpuszcza i jest jak ksiądz,
który bawi się stułą, owijając ją

wokół wskazującego palca.
Ach, gdybyś mógł tak nie paplać,
nie nucić, gdybyś tak mógł nie
zwracać uwagi na zamieszki rasowe,
na zmarszczki i całe to zamieszanie,

które tak chętnie wlewasz w siebie
wraz z lodem, który tonizuje lęk.
Najświeższa panienka kręci tyłkiem
się krzywisz do niej wiedząc, że to śmierć.

PIERWSZY PLAN – CIEMNE UJĘCIE

Dość arktycznie jest tego popołudnia,
tajemnic by się chciało, ale jest obieranie kartofli.
Trzeba gotować, gotować nawet tajemnice.

Pragnienie to tylko karuzela, kurczak
to tajemnica ciała. I przyłapujesz mnie czule
z nożykiem zwieszonym nad wiadrem,
czasami potrafię płakać. Monstra chodzą
obok naszego domu i zaciskają szczęki.

Bardzo żeńskie to zaciskanie.
Bardzo taneczne to chodzenie.

getting stung by a scorpion or some
other reptile. Scales all over the body,
a metamorphosis, or slow dying
from the deformation of my face. Alcohol
disinfects, absolves, and is like the priest
fiddling with his stole, twirling it

around his index finger.
Oh, if only you could stop your chatter,
your blather, if only you could stop
paying attention to the race riots, the
wrinkles, the whole commotion

you're glad to guzzle down
with the ice, which tempers the fear.
The new girl up there shakes her arse,
you grimace at her, knowing it's death.

PLAN A – DARK SEIZURE

It's pretty arctic this afternoon,
what's wanted is secrets, what's got is the peeling of potatoes.
One should cook, cook even the secrets.

Desire is merely a merry-go-round, a chicken
the secret of the body. And you catch me tenderly,
with my knife dangling over the pail.
At times I manage to cry. Monsters walk
alongside our house, clenching their jaws.

How womanly that clenching is,
how danced that walking.

RONDO

Zapisuję zdarzenia
zimy są rodzajem wodospadu
i nie brzmi to absurdalnie.
Złodzieje wydają się
nieruchomym stawem, w którym
znikają przedmioty. Ale słowa
dzieją się tak źle jak oni,
zgarniają nas i na pętli
muszę ci odpowiedzieć:
nic nie mam, zniknęło.

Idziemy do tego domu
który zbudowano na miejscu ogrodu.
Pamiętam wiatr, który
wyginał gałęzie, gdzieś zapisałem
ten wiatr i teraz plącze się w umyśle
drgająca witka leszczyny,
ruchliwa jak oszołomiony węgorz.
Zamiast podłogi gałęzie,
konar zamiast sufitu, sypialnia
pełna zimnych i wilgotnych liści.

Teraz jest tu pusto, dom stracił zęby
dziąsła rozmiękły i mięśnie drżą,
rosa osadza się na niezdrowej skórze.
Linoleum traci połysk za dnia i
budzi się nocą, kurcząc i pękając.
Dzielnica jest zła i złe są urzędy,
zła pogoda i źle dobrane słowa by
opisać ten stan – krzyk orlika
nagrany przez ornitologa, jego
głos jak szron.
Mam suchy język i nie chcę
klepać modlitw. Nawet nie
dochodzimy do furtki, kiedy
zmieniam plan. Lepiej zostać
tutaj. Patrzeć jak na sąsiedniej
parceli kopią fundamenty.

RONDO

I note down events
winters are a kind of waterfall
and that doesn't sound absurd.
Thieves seem
a still pond in which
things disappear. But words
take place as badly as they do,
they round us up and at the last stop
I have to answer you:
I have nothing, it disappeared.

We go to the house
that was built in place of an orchard.
I remember how the wind would splay
the branches, somewhere I noted down
that wind, and now in my thoughts
a quivering twig of hazel lingers,
restless as a stunned eel.
Branches for a floor,
boughs for a ceiling, the bedroom
filled with leaves cold and wet.

Now it is empty here, the house has lost its teeth,
the gums go soft, the muscles tremble,
dew settles on its unhealthy skin.
The linoleum loses its gloss by day and
wakes up at night, shrinking and cracking.
The neighbourhood is bad and bad the municipality,
bad weather and badly chosen words for
describing this state – the eagle's cry
taped by the ornithologist, a
voice like frost.
My tongue is dry and I don't want to
spout litanies. We haven't even
made it to the gate when
I change my plans. Better to stay
here. To watch how they dig
the foundations on the next plot over.

SENNE SANECZKI

Czy mnie potępisz, śpiący między szynami
liściu łopianu,
kiedy się głucho odbijają od ciebie
pomruki pierwszych przechodniów?

Gdybyś się nagle uniósł, mógłbyś całkiem
zakryć tę wiatę na Kórnickiej,
gdzie czekam na szóstkę i wymyślam, co
powiem szefowi, gdy zapyta dlaczego
tak późno przychodzę.

Mógłbyś mnie otulić i zwinąć się jak cygaro,
tak, żebym mógł przeczekać atak mgły
i ten chłód, który się wzmaga i rodzi
podejrzenie, że nie zatrzyma się wcale.

Mógłbyś też (wcale nie żartuję) stać
się tym tajemnym zielem, które daje
przez chwile wrażenie, że jest się bez ciała.
Ale ty jesteś postrzępiony i żółkniesz
w kilku miejscach naraz.
                    Jeszcze kilka
dni i nie zobaczę cię tu wcale; senne saneczki
będą ześlizgiwać się z pagórka,
dzieci ugniotą śnieg wdrapując się pod górę,
będę wsiadał na innym przystanku.

SLUMBERY SLEDS

Will you condemn me,
burdock leaf
asleep between the tracks,
when you mutely reverberate
with the mumbling of the day's first walkers?

If suddenly you rose up, you could cover
this tram stop shelter on Kornicka
where I'm waiting for the number six, thinking
what to tell my boss when he asks why
I'm getting in so late.

You could close up around me, furl like a cigar,
so I can wait out the attack of fog
and this cold, which intensifies and generates
suspicions it will never entirely stop.

You could also (and I'm not joking) turn
into that clandestine weed that gives
the fleeting feeling of not having a body.
But you're ragged and yellowing
in several places at once.
                    A few days
more and I won't see you here at all; slumbery sleds
will ride down the hill,
children pack the snow as they climb up,
I'll be getting in at the other stop.

Translated by W. Martin

CZECH REPUBLIC

PHOTO: MARTIN ŠPELDA

PETR BORKOVEC was born in Lounovice pod
Blaníkem in 1970. A prizewinning author of five
collections of poetry and a translator, he has worked
as editor of the Christian cultural journal *Souvislosti*
(*Connections*) and of the cultural weekly *Literární
noviny*, as well as a publishing editor. His poems have
been translated into many languages, the collections
Field Work and *Needlebook* being published in
German, and selected poems in Italian. Borkovec has
translated Russian twentieth-century poetry
(Khodasevich, Nabokov, Odarchenko, Gippius, Ivanov)
and has collaborated on translations of contemporary
Hungarian poetry, classical Korean poetry and classical
Greek drama *Oedipus Rex* and *Oresteia*.

PETR BORKOVEC

ÓDA

V únoru sýkorka přilétá k ruce s knihou
v okenním rámu, na plátně tepla z topení,
a stojíc bokem, politá peřím, zkamení –
jako by třaslavý hřbet, záblesk hlavy skryla v oku.

Období zimy se jí zuby nehty drží, když tam
tak stojí, neživá, v glazuře – to říkáš ty – peří,
krásná bez prolínání, na vteřinu měřitelná
jen jinými lesklými věcmi, co jsou vidět;

viditelná jen celou blyštivostí, již si měří
rytmy a proporce, tmavé a temné, přelévání
hran a rozestupy ploch, jejichž přirovnání
tě srazí, možná zpátky, k ledovému parapetu.

To oko je jak maska. Čeho? Válčícího mrazu
a lesa, co se na okrajích rozepíná
jak rukáv, skoro ve tmě, který nevystřídá
zápěstí, pěst, jen světlo chladně lámající větve

na horizontu, kam se pohled uhne mezi řečí,
prasklý ret, detail suché ruky, skoro něčí, mokrý
sníh za ramenem na svetru, tající mezi oky,
a borovice s kdoulí v stuze nade dveřmi.

ROZEPSÁNO V DEN SMRTI

Oni se vracejí pro nás, k hromadám našich výdechů,
které se každou noc nachrlí stranou pelesti.

Mezi pootevřenými ústy jim blýská studené sklíčko,
v šatech ušitých na míru čirému dechu

zhášejí svíci a zavírají okno, oběma rukama
do čista uhlazují naše sípající látky.

ODE

A great-tit swoops down to a book held
in February, at a window screened by heat,
and standing side on seems to have just set,
the body's flash and tremor all for its eye.

The winter holds on tooth and nail through it,
stock still, glazed over – as you say – in feathers,
beautiful and distinct, a moment measurable
only by other shining things,

made out by gleam alone, taking the measure
of rhythms and dark ratios, the spillages
of interval and edge – their likeness
knocking you back almost to the icy sill.

That eye's a mask. Of what? Warring frost
and forest open far out to the margins
like sleeves, almost in darkness, with no emerging
wrist or fist, just cold light breaking branches

on the horizon, where gazes go without saying:
chapped lip, someone's dry hand (almost), water
like eyelets from snow melted on a sweater,
and ribboned pine and quince above the door.

NATURAL CAUSES

They're returning for us, to the crowds of our exhalations,
which each night billow forth about the bedframe.

Between half-open mouths they have a cold glass glittering;
in robes cut to a T around sheer breath

they put out candles, close the window, and with both hands
smooth out our wheezing fabrics completely.

* * *

Lyra je lehýnká, nic neváží.
Přes noc se říjen zhroutil na peron,
přiskřípěl pantograf, pryč nádraží,
čtvrthodinový pásovitý skon

za oknem vlaku. Krásný, že až mrazí.
Zelené mraky, topol v modrém stínu,
příměstské pole – Arles na vteřinu.
A když čajové nízké slunce srazí

se s městským vstupem, s okny na kraji
a minutový Betlém spatřím venku,
je lyra lehká tak, že hledám ji
jak jízdní lístek, jako peněženku.

* * *

Stav vody, říční režim, práce, puls
západní strany oblohy teď večer,
v záhybu řeky měkké čtverce vzduchu,
dokud je poslední pták neodvleče.

Z hladiny trčí lávka, kroky,
vrásčitá pláž, skopnuté boty, písek,
co si tě nenápadně prohlíží,
led, co tě prořízne, i tempa. Nevrátí se

nic. Snad rybář v loďce, na obraze,
pozorující odstín svého splávku,
ten, co se shledává už jenom s předměty.
Hřmění a hukot. Otloukají lávku.

* * *

Lighter than light, a lyre weighs nothing.
October in one night comes down.
The train screeches into the station –
then out, a fifteen-minute zone

of passing away. So beautiful:
green clouds, a poplar in blue shadow,
outlying fields – Arles for a moment.
And when the tannin sun falls low

against the town, and a Bethlehem scene
appears an instant along the line,
the lyre is so light that I reach for it
as for my change, as for my ticket out.

* * *

The work, the river's watermark, the swell
of sunset on the west side of the sky.
Soft folds of air caught in the current's turn
for as long as the last bird has yet to fly.

A foot-bridge propped up on the surface, footsteps,
a wrinkled beach, a pair of shoes, and sand,
which watches you discreetly, although withdrawn,
ice, which razors you, strokes. Point

of no return. Man depicted on a punt,
perhaps observing his float's glint and play.
Who now encounters only things themselves.
The roar and thunder. The slim bridge rubbed away.

* * *

Na polích za městem byl sníh, a není,
a přesto chybí pocit rozuzlení,

chuť, pachuť změny, ani ta ne,
když pozoruješ prázdné pláně,

vzdálené, blízké, jako na dlani.
Nad polní zemí letí havrani

jak černá deska, jak stín vzducholodě,
jak jednotvárné vlečné lodě,

táhnoucí po jediné trase
hladinu, která zavírá se,

říční most a dno, říční ostrov, přívoz,
říční břeh, říční mávající život.

Jak černé kopce navršené hřměním
dálnice, jako vnitrozemské změny

počasí, povrchů a světel
na odpočívadlech a v benzinových světech,

tam, kde si stíny zapínají stín,
a reflektory loví fresky propasti.

Jak pohled, který zavřou lesní zdi,
jako les, který průsek odhodí,

jak průsek, který strhne lesní tma,
jak les, jenž pole odrovná,

tak matní jako hloučky laní v poli,
káně na kraji čehokoli

a oko za sklem obrácené za ní.

* * *

Snow general on outlying fields – gone now.
But still no revelation, nothing new:

an aftertaste of change, if that,
when you observe the planes – empty, flat –

and hold the very distance in your hand.
The rooks delight and fly above the land,

a black panel, shadow of an airship;
a string of tugboats uniform in shape

which pulls along the same and single track
the surface, which then coils and closes back,

the river's bridge and bed, the river isle,
the shore, the works and days of river life.

Like black hills crowned with the constant thunder
of a highway, like weather's distant trundle

inland, the shifting brilliancies and planes
at lay-bys and at dirty filling stations,

there where the shadows grade back into murk,
and headlights carve quick frescos from the dark.

Like a gaze blacked out by closing forest walls.
Like the forest broken open by wood trails,

like wood trails which the forest dark then seals,
like the forest razed to leave outlying fields,

as matt as these hinds poised before the sedge,
a beast of prey that stands at something's edge,

and an eye beyond glass that turns behind them.

HŘIŠTĚ ÚL

Myš, list, had a pták –
to z kruhu jejich proměn, co se ozývá
šramocením a sykotem,
je tady kolem všechno uděláno. Rez
pletiva každou chvíli polkne němé slunce,
a vzápětí ji mrak a zvuky znovu propletou.
Vysáté, rozvalené pámely a bezy
vítr už dávno nechal supům světla,
a zdá se, že i ti už odtáhli –
zbloudilý záblesk ohne celý keř.
Nebe je bílé, kluzké, vysypané drtí,
vpravo se zdvíhá spolu se svahem,
vlevo se opatrně spouští nad čtvrť v údolí
do rovnoměrné modři hukotu a hřmění.
A zvíře zraku sebou škube v síti
z jisker a stínů mezi hrušněmi,
tam vzadu, nad hřbitovem míčů.

Strom dělí liják v prostoru a čase
tak jako metrum nezřetelné mumlání
nad šerpou škváry, která přetíná
antukový kurt, ztvrdlý na kachle.
Neudržíš to v sobě ani vteřinu;
už zasyčení, šramot slova, prostě to,
co jenom pozoruješ – možná míň:
přecházíš očima – tak jako věc,
která se třeba sune k ruce, sebere
studený cizí takt a strčí do pece.
Na stožár v písku, promíchaném
s šlahouny břečťanu a zasvištěním lanka,
je napíchnutá větev akátu,
do které vráží šedobílou lajnu
neviditelné letadlo. Déšť ztichl, naráz,
bez příčiny – jak přesný letargický stroj.
A odevšad teď malé lesklé stroje.

Schodiště stoupá, rozříznuté
červeným zábradlím, přeseknuté
silnicí o pár metrů výš.
Obrubní dílce schodů, vystouplé,
hladké a hrbolaté jako dásně.
Nahoru míří vidlice průseků,
odsunují se, zasunují,

HONEYCOMB PLAYGROUND

Mouse, leaf, snake and bird –
out of the ring of their changes, what calls
(whispering, rustling, hissing)
has fashioned everything around. Rust
on wiring is swallowed by the sun each moment,
then clouds and noise knit it back again.
Buck-bushes, lean elders, are lying round,
left to the light's great vultures long ago,
and even they seem to have drifted off.
A wayward bolt of lightning twists a bush.
The sky is white, slippery, grading into grain –
on the right, it rises with the slope,
on the left, it swoops carefully down over the streets,
an even blue, all roar and thunder.
The sparks and shadows in between the pear-trees
net my whole vision, as they would a beast
a small way off, down where the balls roll to a stop.

In space and time, a tree divides the downpour
as metre does the low, muddy murmurs
above the swirls of slag that run and flow
over the hardened *en tout cas*, baked like tiles.
You cannot hold it in you, even for a moment,
this hissing, gradual rustle of a word, the thing
so bare your eyes are watching (or maybe only
drifting over) – just as you would
something which, say, shunts into the hand,
takes up the strange rhythm, and fires it into stone.
The sand is mixed with twists of ivy
and trilling wire. There's a pole on which
a branch of acacia is firmly fixed,
and into this there thrusts the grey-white line
of an unseen airplane. The rain went quiet, suddenly,
without cause – like an exact lethargic machine.
And from everywhere now the small glossy machines.

The steps rise upwards, cut across
by a red railing, and then a little higher
truncated by a road.
The kerb of the steps, raised,
smooth, and contoured like a gum.
The paths fork, head up and off,
drift and shift aside, away,

a každý je ukončen vzpomínkou:
nárožní vížka, tholon, kjótský altán.
Drnčící lanko, schody, jméno ulice
si bez ustání prohazují místo.
V serpentýně se mačká suchá tráva,
ponořená až na dno svého živoření.
A na ní cize spočívá
dřevěná bedna s pískem a solí,
tak beztížně, že se zdá, jako by
povodeň ještě neopadla.

U zídky plotu sbíráš mokrý papír,
rozpitý, v půlce přeložený seznam
příjmení nebo věcí. Nejspíš příjmení
školáků nebo hráčů, možná herců.
Zasychá v kapse. Jdeš dál, nahoru,
pak vlevo kolem lesní zahrady.
Čtvrť za zády se vrství, překrývá,
nečitelná, vodově modrá. Ale
neohlížíš se, ani jednou ne,
jako bys nesměl a jako bys musel
šlapat jen na určené kostky
v rytmických ornamentech dláždění.

and each ends with a memory:
a corner turret, *tholos*, Kyoto bower.
The whipping wire, the steps, the streetname
swap places ceaselessly with one another.
On the snaking paths the grass is clumped
and pressed down to its frail roots.
And on it, strangely,
rests a wooden chest with sand and salt,
so weightlessly that it seems as if
the flood had not yet ebbed.

Near the fence you pick up a piece of paper,
folded in two, wet through, the ink running,
a list of names or things. Most likely names
of schoolchildren, a team, or maybe actors.
Pocketed, it slowly dries. You go on, and up,
then left around a garden amongst the trees.
Behind, the streets are layered on one another
illegibly, a kind of watery blue. But even then
you don't look back once,
as though you shouldn't, and as though you must
plant your feet on certain squares
in the pavement's rhythmic ornaments.

Translated by Justin Quinn

PHOTO: KAREL CUDLÍN

KATEŘINA RUDČENKOVÁ was born in Prague in 1976 and studied at the Jaroslav Ježek Conservatoire and at the Faculty of Economics and Management in Prague. Since 1998 she has published poetry in Czech dailies and literary magazines. She is editor of the cultural internet magazine *Dobrá adresa*.

Her first collection *Ludwig* was published to general acclaim in 1999. Her second book *No Need for You to Visit Me* came out in 2002, and *Nights, Nights* in 2004. A bilingual book of her poetry *Nicht nötig, mich zu besuchen* was published by Wieser Verlag in Austria in 2002. Kateřina Rudčenková lives in Prague.

KATEŘINA RUDČENKOVÁ

* * *

Co bych dal za to, aby Achmatovová sestoupila
z Petrov-Vodkinova obrazu, zatímco by stále tak
na mne hleděla... lehla by si vedle mě
ve tmě.

Na jaře ke mně sestupují jen touhy
Zbývá mi vpíjet se do věcí

*"Na jaře se všichni ptáci
vracejí do Bibireva."*

*„Pamatuješ, jak jsem ti na Vyhlídce
ukazovala toho muže v čele stolu?"*

Okouzlení přímou řečí.

NIKDE

Obrostu fialovými listy,
kořeny nechám pod vodou.

Otevřeš okna, dolehnou k tobě
rány palice, jak tu v zimě
u kádí zabíjeli kapry.

Začteš se, budeš se zaobírat věcmi,
abys nemyslela na sebe.

V hlasech ti bude dobře,
zbydou dvě věty,
první z mého, druhá
z tvého žebra.

* * *

I'd give anything for Akhmatova to step down
from Petrov-Vodkin's picture, and, continuing to fix me
with that gaze… lie down by my side
in the dark.

In spring I am visited only by desires
Nothing left to do but lose myself in things.

*"In spring, all the birds
return to Bibirevo."*

*"Do you remember me showing you that man
sitting at the head of the table in the Belvedere?"*

Enchanted by direct speech.

NOWHERE

Covered by purple leaves
I'll leave my roots under water.

You will open the windows, and from a distance
hear the blows from the time when
they killed carp by the vats in winter.

You will immerse yourself in reading, pondering things
so as not to think about yourself.

You will feel good inside those voices,
with two sentences left,
the first made of my rib,
the second of yours.

NOCI

Zejména teplé noci s okny dokořán
jsou naplněny výkřiky a vzlyky.

Skrz korunu není vidět příchozích.
Tenhle rok tady končí.

Student, který je na ulici chodcem
a v moři tonoucím,
se stane maličkým svatým
v nějakém rodinném výklenku.

Tak a je noc. Poznáš mě
podle kroků a tvaru stínu.

* * *

Žena ve vlaku, která ke svému
jedinému synovi mluvila jako k milenci.

Dotyk loktů. Krátké povzdechnutí.

"Nesněz to všechno. Pojedeme za tmy."

* * *

Ano, já bydlím v klavíru,
ale není nutné,
abyste mě navštěvoval.

NIGHTS

Mostly warm nights with windows open wide
are filled with cries and sobs.

Visitors are invisible through treetops.
This is where the year draws to an end.

A student, who is a pedestrian in the street
and a drowning man at sea,
becomes a tiny saint
in some family alcove.

There, the night has come. You'll know me
by my footsteps and by the shape of my shadow.

* * *

A woman on the train, talking
to her only son as if to a lover.

Elbows touching. A brief sigh.

"Don't eat it all. We'll travel in the dark."

* * *

Yes, I live inside the piano.
but there is no need for you
to come and visit me.

* * *

Těším se na spánek
jako by bylo možné jím vycouvat
ze života

Večer je vyhrazen ženám
Přimknout se těsně, dusivě

Ještě to vydrž, slibují
jako by bylo na co čekat

NÁVŠTĚVA V SANATORIU

Gertruda si mě vezme stranou
svěřujíc mi rukopisy vytažené z ohně.

Na stěně tančí ancistrus
a její stín, když mě prosí
– řekněte mu, že se nejmenuji Berta!

Z ramen si střásá prachové brouky.
– Berto… mluví s vámi někdy
aniž by blouznil?

Rozražené okno, terasa
plná holubů, živočišný vír. Dál
Gertruda už jen významě mlčí,
terasa povolila, pokoj vzplál.

* * *

I look forward to sleep
as if it allowed us to back out of life.

Evening is reserved for women.
A tight, stifling embrace.

Bear it a little longer, they promise
as if there were something to wait for.

A VISIT TO THE SANATORIUM

Gertrude takes me aside
entrusting me with manuscripts rescued from the fire.

An ancistrus dances on the wall
and her shadow, as she begs me
– tell him that my name is not Bertha!

Shaking off dust insects from her shoulders
– Bertha… does he ever talk to you
without raving?

A gaping window, a terrace
full of pigeons, animal vortex, then
nothing but Gertrude's charged silence
the terrace sinks, the room goes up in flames.

LUNYI SVĚT

Hlavy jak lampy *anglepoise*
Tvář stejné barvy v pozadí
Prosvětlený les
V tom lese hřbitov obehnaný
      bílou zdí
Pokrytý poledními stíny
Z nichž žádné nedosáhnou
      ke kostelu
A okna, okna na večerní způsob

To všechno během jediného
      otočení hlavou
anglepoise, anglepoise
Jaké to asi je, být sežrán
      zvířecí tlamou?

LUNYI SVET*

Heads like anglepoise lamps
A face the same colour in the background
A luminescent forest
In it a white-walled
          cemetery
Covered with noon shadows
None of which reaches
          as far as the church
And windows, evening-like windows

All that in a single
          turn of the head
Anglepoise, anglepoise
What does it feel like
to be devoured
          in the jaws of a beast?

Translated by Alexandra Büchler

* 'Moon World' or 'Moon Light' in Russian

SLOVAKIA

PHOTO: PETER BALCAR

KATARÍNA KUCBELOVÁ was born in 1979 in Banská Bystrica, Slovakia and studied at the Academy of Dramatic Art, Bratislava, Department of Film and Television Art where she obtained an MA in screen-writing.

Two of her screenplays have been made into short films, one of which she directed and her first collection of poetry, *Duály (Duals)* was published in 2003. Her work – poetry, prose and film reviews – has appeared in a number of Slovakian, Czech and Hungarian literary magazines. She is currently working as a script editor.

KATARÍNA KUCBELOVÁ

* * *

hladina preniká do hladiny

pretekanie
:premiestňovanie dotýkaním:

(dokonalý pohyb)

úsilie nemať
tvar

:dokonalé umiestnenie:

nezastaviť

* * *

prijímať

v jednoduchom procese výberu
prestávam klásť odpor: prestávam spolupracovať

(urči najjednoduchšie)

X
on je □
on urobil □

prijímať znášať
príčiny

prijímať byť
v pohybe

* * *

surface penetrating surface

overflow
:rearranging through touching:

(*a perfect movement*)

the effort not to have
a face

:a perfect placing:

unceasing

* * *

accepting

in the simple process of choice
I stop resisting: I stop co-operating

(specify the simplest)

	X
he is	☐
he did	☐

accepting causing
reasons

accepting being
in movement

* * *

: podstatná v celku:
: obsiahnutá v hladine:
: prítomnosť vymedzená dotykom:
: hladina sa dotýka hladiny:
: tvorený mnou: tvorená tebou:
: samostatne nečitateľná:

* * *

I

skúšanie

bod ktorý je vzdialený ale viditeľný
neviditeľný nahmatateľý
vzdialený

namáhavé napodobňovanie

hľadanie
(len) pokusom
o dokonalosť môžeme vytvoriť nedokonalosť
nedokonalosť: pohyb

skúšanie

(dokonalý)

: potreba vytvoriť vzor
: potreba vytvoriť pohyb

:potreba nedokonalosti:

* * *

:essential in the whole:
:clasped in the surface:
:presence limited by touch:
:surface touches surface:
:created by me: created by you:
:separately unreadable:

* * *

I

scrutinising

a point that is far away yet visible
invisible untouchable
far away

strenuous imitating

searching
(only) by experiment
on perfection we can create imperfection
imperfection: movement

scrutinising

(perfect)

:the need to create the ideal
:the need to create movement

:the need for imperfection:

* * *

II

(vzory:)

; dokonalý – dokonalejší;
; skoro dokonalý – dokonalý;

dva: (od: k) *(pohyb)*

zdanlivo dvojité: zdanlivo jedno

:nekonečné približovanie:

dokonalý vzor potrebuje dokonalý vzor

* * *

zauzlenie

predpokladá dotyk
z dotyku vyplýva vzrušenie

dotyku predchádza spojenie: spojenie je vzťah
vzťah sa nekončí oddelením

spojenie spôsobuje zmenu
smeru *ktorú nemusí narušiť zotrvačnosť*

ktorú pred ním nemožno predpovedať

podstatný je moment prekvapenia
určujúci je proces očakávania
(momentu prekvapenia)

jeho intenzitu určuje nevyspytateľnosť zmeny

* * *

II

(ideals:)

;perfect – more perfect;
;almost perfect – perfect;

two: (from; to) *(movement)*

deceptively double: deceptively one

:unendingly approximating:

a perfect ideal needs a perfect ideal

* * *

entanglement

anticipated touch
from touch comes arousal

joining precedes touch: joining is relationship
                              relationship does not end with disconnecting

joining causes a change
              of direction   *which needn't be violated by inertia*

which can't be predicted

essential the moment of astonishment
determinate the process of expectation
              (the moment of astonishment)

its intensity is determined by the inability to predict change

z toho vyplýva vzrušenie
je to príjemné   *(je to príjemné)*

                                        vzťah sa nezačína spojením

dotyky sa obnovujú
podnet je vzrušenie
a vzrušenie je príjemné
prostriedok je zmena
zmena sa vytvorí dotykom

                                        vzťah sa nekončí oddelením

každý dotyk nesie v sebe zmenu

ktorá sa udiala
ktorá sa udeje

                                        dotyk je spojenie: spojenie je vzťah
                                        zmenu smeru nemusí narušiť zotrvačnosť

každá zmena nesie v sebe dotyk
tento pohyb je utkvený v bode
smer nemožno predpovedať
                                        z toho vyplýva vzrušenie

 ja poviem nie
    ty áno
 a vlastne
    nesúhlasíš

from this comes arousal
it is pleasant   *(it is pleasant)*

                              relationship does not begin with joining

touches are renewed
impulse is arousal
and arousal is pleasant
the medium is change
change is created by touch
                    relationship does not end with disconnection

every touch bears change within itself

which had happened
which will happen

                    touch is joining: joining is relationship
                    a change of direction needn't be violated
                                        by inertia

every change bears touch within itself
this movement is attached to a point
a direction cannot be predicted
                    from this comes arousal
I say no
    you yes
and you really
    disagree

* * *

rozuzlenie

predpokladá začiatok
        začiatok definuje koniec

(a dĺžka trvania napĺňa existenciu motiváciou)

právoplatnosť projekcie
                neuskutočnených možností

predpokladá začiatok a začiatok definuje koniec

neurčitosť projekcie
                uskutočnených možností

ktorýkoľvek bod projekcie
je zároveň bodom
začiatku aj konca

a dĺžka trvania napĺňa existenciu motiváciou

ja poviem nie
    ty áno
a vlastne
    nesúhlasíš

* * *

denouement

anticipated beginning
   beginning defines the end

(and the length of persistence fills existence with motivation)

the lawfulness of the projection
        of unexperienced possibilities

anticipated beginning and beginning defines the end

the indefiniteness of the projection
        of experienced possibilities

any point of projection
is at the same time a point
of beginning and end

and the length of persistence fills existence with motivation

I say no
  you yes
and you really
  don't agree

* * *

robiť len nepatrné
pohyby nevyrušiť

ich

pod hladinou

neupozorniť

nad hladinou

ponúka sa: splynúť
synonymum pre
dávať aj brať

zároveň

lynúť

mohlo byť výhodným riešením
nebyť
rizika obnovovania

* * *

pokračovať
až kým sa stratí
význam

pokračovať

a potom:

pokračovať

až kým sa stratí pojem

pokračovať

neprestať aby nevzniklo

prázdne miesto: potreba

nahradiť

pokračovať / neprestať
aby zánik bol dokonalý
nesmie byť konečný

* * *

making just insignificant
movements not to disturb

        them

under the surface

        not warning

above the surface

offers itself: integrating
synonym for
giving and for taking

at the same

        integrating

could have been a convenient solution
had there not been
a risk of renewing

* * *

continuing
until meaning
is lost

        continuing

and then:

continuing

until concept is lost

continuing

        not stopping so it will come into existence

empty places: need

replacing

continuing / not stopping
so extinction will be perfect
it is not permitted to be finished

        Translated by James Sutherland-Smith
        and Katerina Sutherland-Smithová

PHOTO: AUTHOR'S ARCHIVE

MARTIN SOLOTRUK was born in 1970 in Bratislava and obtained an MA in English and Slovak, and a PhD on American Poetry from the Comenius University, Bratislava, where he now teaches.

His first book of poetry, *Tiché vojny* (*Silent Wars*), won the Slovak Literary Fund Best Debut Award in 1997, and his second collection, *Mletie*, was published in 2001. He is also known as a translator, and his translations of the poetry of, among others, Ted Hughes, John Ashbery, Seamus Heaney and Charles Simic have appeared in book form and in magazines in Slovakia.

MARTIN SOLOTRUK

**MYDLO SA MUSELO STAŤ MOJÍM
ŽIVOTNÝM KRÉDOM, KEĎŽE SOM
NAŠIEL VAŇU TAM, KDE NEMALA
BYŤ ANI ŠTRBINKA, NIČ**

Neutkviem, neuviaznem medzi vecami,
                pokým sa snažím držať mydla.

Nemusím ani veriť,
a robí čisto na vznikajúcej oblohe,

cez ultracitlivý filter vzduchu pomáha
tomu, čo má vstúpiť
do môjho sveta.

Mám stále čas
skákania cez švihadlo,
vykľúvajúci a vkľúvajúci sa.

Len niekedy, keď je to možno na niečo potrebné,
mi do toho neosobné, ani nezhrdelnené zvýsknutie
prerazí zovretie preglgnutia naprázdno
                s troškou slinky,
upovedomí ma,
že týmto kanálikom
môžem ešte predposunkovo hovoriť
s odídenými, vytrácajúcimi sa,
obrovitánskymi oblakmi,
keď som si už tadiaľ aj tak raz uvedomil
ich neustávajúcu prítomnosť.

Nič na tom nezmení ani zadutie,
hoci by v ňom i bol závan slobody, kolembania
nôh v rytme inom než pochod
na podobné príkazy, o ktorých sa nediskutuje.

Konečne
teda prišlo na ja-blko.

Našlo si dlho zapotrošenú čiernu korunku
vo vnútri v sebe
a ešte ho i hrklo,
že je to impulz.

THE SOAP HAD TO BECOME MY CREED
AS I FOUND A BATHTUB
WHERE THERE WAS SUPPOSED TO BE
NEITHER NOOK NOR CRANNY

I won't get attached, entangled among things
                    while I try to hold on to the soap.

I'm not even a believer,
and it washes the emerging sky clean

through an ultra-sensitive air filter aiding
what has to enter
my world.

I always enjoy time
skipping the rope
waxing and waning.

Only sometimes, if perhaps there is something needed,
cut by an, impersonal to me, not even consonantal cry
blowing open in vain a sudden gulp
                  with a little spit,
enlightening me
that through this channel
I can still prelinguistically speak
with fleeing, dwindling
enormous clouds
when I've once been made aware
of their nebulous presence.

It's set. Nothing changes even by a blow
although it might be a free gust, rolling
its legs in a rhythm different from a run
of a kind similar to that which can't be discussed.

Eventually
it comes to the apple of one's I.

All at once a long lost black crown is found
right there within itself
and even gets the jolt
that it is an impulse.

Odvtedy sa vydá kamkoľvek
a okolie v protismere vystrája,
tak trochu vnucuje
prehliadku, pocty, ktoré ono jablko musí
vo vlastnom záujme prehliadnuť
hneď ďalším prekopŕcnutím.

Je to sled sledovania sa,
Avšak naše pohlavia si už dávno našli čosi spoločné,
čosi, čo ich vydeľuje z radu, zástupu, zastupiteľnosti.

Tak sa nám v tomto čase, teraz, na vrchole vzájomného leta,
keď akýkoľvek ďalší pohyb
už iba pomieša hrušky s jablkami,
začína vo farebných prelietavých škvrnkách,
hmýrení v pote
        i príležitostnom šteku
prejavovať šokujúci obranný reflex
osvojeného slnka.

**NECH BEŽÍM KAMKOĽVEK, VŽDY ZOSTÁVAM
NA BICYKLI, ABY SOM SA V CIELI VYHOL
ZMÄTKOM PRI JEHO PREDAJI NA SÚČIASTKY**

… bicykle chodia okolo,
dotvárajú nás,
skúšajú, či v momente vykročenia nie sme vedení zmyslom
pre povinnosť.

Krok tak ako vzniká, aj zaniká,
žiadnemu z nich by som sa neodvážil hádať vek.

Takto vnášam nové momenty
do už skončených pátraní po zmysle, neodvolateľnosti
a tichého gesta vznešenosti týchto zdomácnených kolies,
ktoré si však nenápadne

vo svojom strede, ložiskách uchovávajú
všetko z nerozanalyzovateľnej pôvodnosti.

Since then it weds wherever,
rolling against hail,
thus slightly grand-daughtering
an oversight, honour, which the apple must
in its own interest overlook
immediately in further somersaults.

It's a sequence to be followed.
Yet our genitals have long since found something together,
something that excludes them from the ranks, masses and substitution.

So now in our time at the height of summer
when any further motion
has only shaken apples and pears
it begins in coloured, transparent specks,
a buzzing in our sweat
                also a random barking
manifesting in us a shockingly defensive reflex
of the adopted sun.

**WHEREVER I RUN I ALWAYS STAY
ON A BICYCLE SO AS TO PREVENT ANY
CONFUSION ABOUT ITS SALE FOR SPARE PARTS**

… bicycles move around
completing us
testing whether at the moment of advancing we are led by a sense
of duty.

As a step is extinguished as it is conceived
I wouldn't dare guess the age of any of them.

Thus I introduce new moments
into already concluded searches for sense, irreversibility
and a quiet gesture of grace in these domesticated wheels
which, however unnoticed,

in their centre, in their bearings maintain
all of their unanalysable originality.

Niekoľko zádrheľov a následných pokľaknutí po sebe
niekedy vyvoláva dohady o vzniku novej školy, hnutia,

no tieto prvým výstrelom nenávratne miznú,
už nie je na ne čas.
Zostáva len beh,
pnutie a delenie šiestym zmyslom pulzujúcich buniek.
Slabšie srdiečka nemajú nárok,
nikdy nedobehnú až tam, až pod správny transparent.

ZLÝ VTIP

Všetko sa to začína už ráno v kúpeľni.

Voľne prúdiaca voda upúta moju pozornosť,
zasiahne do môjho správania
na premenlivú dobu.
A keby som predsa len podcenil svoju kondíciu,
kohútiky,
ktorými sa dá presne nastaviť rýchlosť, miesto, čas,
sú stále na dosah
a dávajú mi možnosť,
aby som sa cítil pánom tejto vždy náhodnej situácie,
pre ktorú odkrývam paplón,
pod ktorým som po mnoho hodín
v tme všeličo zohrieval, potajme dýchal.

Práve tam, kde sme najspontánnejší,
zostávajú po nás fŕkance.
Pre druhých celkom nepoužiteľné,
vyžadujú si zvýšenú opatrnosť.

Veci neznalým sa odporúča na dohodnuté miesta nechodiť,
aby sa do zrkadla,
ktoré iným priznáva všetky výsady kráľov,
nemuseli pozrieť až po tom,
čo si kvôli istej nepredvídavosti o umývadlo odbijú
z korunky.

A few chain hitches and consequent genuflections one after the other
sometimes summoning up theories of the rise of a new school, movement,

but at first shot they vanish irrevocably
in no time at all.
Only the run remains
the flow and division of cells pulsing with a sixth sense.
Weaker hearts don't stand the ghost of a chance
they'll never run all the way under a proper banner.

A BAD JOKE

Everything begins in the morning in the bathroom.

Freely flowing water floods my attention,
affects my behaviour
in a changeable era.
And even should I merely underestimate my condition,
the taps,
which have been set precisely for speed, place, time,
are always within reach
and give me the opportunity
to feel master of this random situation
for which I pull off the quilt
under which I have for many hours
been willy-nilly nesting, secretly breathing.

Right there where we are most spontaneous
we leave behind us spatterings.
For others utterly unusable
they call for the utmost care.

The unknowing are advised not to go to the agreed place
so that in the mirror,
granting all prerogatives to others,
they needn't just see their crown
chipped by a basin.

EŠTE NA VOĽNOM VZDUCHU
EŠTE PRED ZALOŽENÍM DOMÁCNOSTI

My sa naozaj niektoré večery po svojom modlíme,
asi do pol
holého pása zakrytí myslievame jeden pred druhým.

… a zostaneme osamelí, až kým medzi nás
nevhupne kvapka,
niečo ako spoločný zážitok,

zhrčí nás dokopy
do jedného plodu,
aký môže potratiť len panna
ešte predtým;
než odpraceme všetok použitý príbor,
je tu šanca sa porozprávať
z očí do očí,
nadviazať na spolu zažité
hmýrenie
všade tam dolu – až po hranicu viditeľnosti,
a pritom by nešlo o nič odpozorované,
prenesené pohľadom z vonku dnu,

kde sa štvornožky na dlážke ešte nehrajú
deti v pyžamách…

povieme si potom,

veď po kolotočoch býva najviac zhôd okolností

a tu, kde sa končí súvislosť štrbiny,
začína masív…

AGAIN IN THE OPEN AIR
AGAIN BEFORE SETTING UP A HOUSEHOLD

Indeed some evenings we pray
almost half
naked to the waist, we think ourselves into one another.

… and we remain alone while among us
a drop bounces,
something like a mutual experience,

it gnarls us together
into a single fruit
that only a virgin could ever
abort;
all the used cutlery is cleared away,
there's still the chance to talk
eye to eye
to resume the mutually felt
teeming
everywhere below – to the limits of visibility
which is nothing reflected back
of a view from the outside in.

Where pyjama-clad children have yet to play
on all fours on the floor… .

we'll see later

since after the carousels there are more coincidences

and here where the completion of a crevice ends
a massif begins…

Translated by the author and
James Sutherland-Smith

SLOVENIA

PHOTO: GORDANA BOBOJEVIČ

PRIMOŽ ČUČNIK was born in Ljubljana in 1971 and studied philosophy and cultural sociology at Ljubljana Faculty of Arts.

His first collection of poetry, *Two Winters*, was published in 1999 and received Best First Collection Award. His most recent books are *Rhythm in hands* (2002), *Chords* (2004) and *Ode on Manhattan Avenue* (2003), which he co-wrote with Gregor Podlogar. Čučnik translates from Polish, writes literary criticism, book reviews, works as an editor for the magazine *Literatura*, and runs a small press, Sherpa. He lives in Ljubljana.

PRIMOŽ ČUČNIK

VELIKI TIŠINI

I

Tihe strmine, burja buči v dolino,
osojne ulice in v bobničih
odzvanjajoča glasba, ki razbija
radostno tišino in se zajeda v žensko,

moškega, da jo poslušata in stisneta
v objem, tja, kamor topel zrak
nosi spremembo, v mrzle kraje,
ki so v mislih, ko se ljubita, dokler

vročina ne pojenja in se poleže
cestni hrup, kaos veleblagovnic,
ki ne zamenjajo in potolažijo samote,
tako kot glasba v neizurjenih ušesih

ne preglasi razbijanja prometnih
gneč, zavijanja siren ali gibkih
stanj končnih teles in stalnih
položajev zvezd v jasnih nočeh.

II

Rad bi se približal, a tvoja glasba je
tako oddaljena, da je ne ujame uho,
in to kar vrti radio, ni primerljivo,
slab izbor na običajen dan,

ko je vse, kar slišim, drugačna,
nerazložljiva aritmična tišina,
v mojih nevajenih ušesih, sluh,
ki nemo preži, ko avtomobili ugašajo

motorje in monotoni ritmi stroja
iz garaže nehajo udarjati in ni prijetnih
rok na tipkah, po katerih zaigraš kar
koli, nikdar ne prepoznam melodije,

a kar hoče biti slišano je slišano, in se
vrti, sam pa bi prej poslušal tisto, česar ni,
zato sezujem čevlje, stopim v reko,
se zlijem z mimobežnimi stvarmi.

TO A GREAT SILENCE

I

Silent slopes, north wind roars into the valley,
sunless streets, and in the eardrums
music echoes, it shatters
the joyful silence, eats into a woman,

a man, makes them listen and
embrace it where the warm air
carries change, into cold places that are
in our thoughts when making love, until

the heat drops and the street noise
subsides: supermarket chaos
that won't change or comfort solitude
just as music in untrained ears

can't drown the din of traffic,
the wailing of sirens, maleable
states of finite bodies of the fixed
position of stars on a clear night.

II

I want to get closer, but so distant
is your music that one's ear won't hold it,
and what's played on the radio can't compare,
a bad choice on an ordinary day

when everything I hear is different,
inexplicable arythmic silence
ringing in my unaccustomed ears, hearing
lurks deftly when the cars turn off

their engines and the monotony of the machine
in the garage stops pounding, and there are no pleasant
hands on the keys on which you play
anything, and I never recognize the tune,

but what wants to be heard is heard and it
plays and I would rather listen to what is not,
so I take off my shoes, step into the river
and merge with whatever passes.

III

In nekateri pravijo, da je še druga, višja
glasba, ki naj ji prisluhnemo, če bi
hoteli slišati, vendar razen z molkom,
ni dobro odgovarjati hrupni tišini;

torej naj bodo tvoje roke čiste in
ženske, moški objeti, delavci, zgoraj,
varni pred padci in vozniki
obvarovani nesreč, glasbeniki naj

zaslišijo svoje inštrumente v točnem
tonu in enako stori s tistimi,
ki so na ulici, posluh nasloni na
zidove in prisluhni bitju skritega

središča, naj zazveni urbano, ker pri
svojem padcu bi bili radi popolni,
zato ne razdiraj naše izjemnosti,
ki jo slavim v čuječi poeziji.

SPOZNANJE

Vidimkaj se je zgodilo. Poezija je iz mene naredila
pošast. Strašim v spanju, strašim pomirjene. Zbujam
se sredi noči. Ker sem nežen, ker se speči ustrašijo
prikazni mojega drugega jaza. Imena, ki ga črkujem

na izust. In zmeraj glasneje, bolj razločno čutim:
To je moje drugo življenje, prestopil sem mejo
samega sebe. Zmeraj močneje čutim: To je moja
druga smrt. Blazinice se me dotikajo, po obrazu

me božajo, stiskajo me trepalnice jezika, klešče
zgodovine, to razbeljeno železo kovačev.
In vsak glas me predrami, vsak dan prehodim
isto pot, kjer podkve jezika puščajo sledi.

III

And some say that there is another higher
sort of music we should listen to, if we
want to hear, but unless we're quiet,
we don't answer the noisy silence, so

may your hands be clean and
female, men embraced, workers
safe from falls, and drivers
protected from accidents, let musicans

hear their instruments in precise
tones and do the same with those
on the street, lean your ear
against the walls and listen to the hidden

centre, let it ring in the city,
for in our fall we want to be perfect,
so don't dismantle the exceptional
which I celebrate in vigilant poetry.

Translated by Ana Jelnikar and Joshua Beckman

PERCEPTION

I can see what has happened. Poetry has turned me into
a monster. I haunt my own sleep, I haunt those who are calm.
I awake in the middle of the night. Since I am gentle, those
asleep get startled by the apparition of my other being. The name

I spell by heart. And all the more piercingly and distinctly do
I feel: This is my other life, I have outdone
myself. Ever stronger do I feel: This is my
other death. Fingers are touching me, brushing over my face.

I am being crushed by the eyelashes of language, the pincers
of history, the white-hot iron of blacksmiths.
And every voice rouses me, every day I walk the same
path, where the horseshoes of language leave their marks.

Poezija je iz mene naredila stezo. Sledim si
v spanju, hodim za svojo senco. Moje življenje
se pokriva z življenjem juter, ki jih čakam.
Živeti pesniško povzema vsa razpoloženja.

Besede so muka in dar. Zmaga in poraz.
Edino in odveč.

PRVA PESEM

Prva pesem govori o starem načinu
življenja. Kako so bile stvari postavljene
v začetku in kako se je vedelo, kje naj bi
se končale, ali v obrisih ponovno začele

z znanimi čustvi. A potem prične
kukavica biti večje ure, in trava rase
višje in rože cvetijo lepše in popoldanski
sprehajalci se zazirajo v prezrte barve.

Sneg je še bel, ampak bolj čist
in jasen, nebo nad strešniki še modro,
ampak modro v zlatosti odličnega
opoldneva, in pesem še vedno odmevna

v svojem zimzelenem tonu. Zvezde
pogledujejo proti nam kot presenečeni
znanci, srečani spet po tisoč letih
in knjiga še po tisoč letih trdi svoje

in posebna reka se je splazila med
bleščeče kamne, obrušene od stare
rečnosti in pravih oblik, kot trpežna
srca posejanih po dnu njenega rokava.

Ni kak mesec, ki bi se ga dalo imenovati,
ali leto, za katero bi se vedelo, kdaj
se je začelo, so le v uho se zlivajoči
zvoki hipov, ko se ne ve za čas, kot da

Poetry has turned me into a trail. I follow myself
in my sleep, I walk behind my own shadow. My life
is superimposed over the life of mornings I am awaiting.
To live as a poet encompasses all moods.

Words are a torment and a gift. Victory and defeat.
Everything and everything not needed.

FIRST SONG

First song speaks of the old way
of life. How things were set
in the beginning and how it was clear where
they should end or outlined begin again

with familiar feelings. But then the cuckoo
began to strike greater hours, and grass
grew taller and flowers blossomed more beautifully
and afternoon strollers gazed at hitherto missed colours.

Snow still white, but cleaner
and brighter, the sky above the roof tiles still blue,
but blue in the goldenness of a perfect
afternoon, and the song still resounding

in its evergreen tones. The stars cast
their glance towards us like surprised acquaintances
bumping into one another after a thousand years,
and the book sticks to its claim even after a thousand years

and a special river has crawled between
the glittering rocks from the old riverness
polished to perfect shapes like durable
hearts tossed into its winding.

Not a month to name
nor a year to know when
it all started, only sounds of moments
poured into an ear and the time unknown

bi bil ves čas preteklost, tvoj izvirni greh
je zakopan še v spanju in iz praznih
žepov še lahko potegneš prvo pesem,
ki te ponese tja. A zdaj je jasna in razločna,

le njen refren, ki si ga enkrat znal na pamet,
se spreminja, da nikoli ne ujameš besed.

* * *

Izvlečem in obrnem ključ v vratih na Gosposki, kjer že
prej na zid prislonim kolo in vstopim, snamem ključek,
da bi preveril pošto in v nabiralniku polnem kuvert
se zasveti Tvoje srce, prestrežem še zvonjenje telefona,
ampak poslano vseeno ni za objavo in nekaj je treba
odnest na pošto, nekaj je treba pustit v knjigarni,
ob poldne bom že v galeriji, kjer zadiši kava brez
in v njej zrno sladkorja za grenke dni, ko mimo hitijo
skrbno obriti, počesani, dirjajoči za častmi, seveda,
prerivanja ne bo konec, ne v službi ne v politiki.
Ošvrknem kazalec, mogoče še ujamem Podlogarja z boni
za kosilo, ja, danes bom vzel samo pol porcije,
saj so nahranila že vsa srca, ki se svetijo v nabiralnikih,
na pločnikih in zataknjena v režah granitnih kock,
pa čeprav nisem našel ključa do Tvojih prsi (in tam
izgubljenega srca), bi vseeno poskušal nekaj
norega: ujeti kak trenutek v množici, prestreči
dekličin pogled, sok ženske ali vreči cifro-moža,
ki bo zadostovala do jutri, ko bom spet obrnil
ključavnico in mogoče našel skrivnostno enačbo
najine neustavljive privlačnosti, in bo neko novo srce
postalo cilj hitrosti sodobnega sveta – tukaj,
sredi navidezne blaginje srečnih, ki pečatijo
svoje nekdanje, oh, pretekle in minule bitke,
je vaš utrip kot komaj čuten objem, ki obljublja,
da se tudi na drugi strani vrat ne bo razklenil!

as though all time was past, your original sin
still buried in your sleep, and from an empty
pocket you could pull your first song
which took you there. But it is plain and clear now,

only its chorus that you once knew by heart
keeps changing, so that you can never catch the words.

* * *

I take out and turn the key in Gosposka Street, I've leaned
my bike beside the door and entered, seizing the little key, I
check the box and there, sitting among a bunch of envelopes
is Your shining heart, just in time for the ringing phone,
but all the same what's been sent shouldn't be published, and
a few things need posting, others can stay in the bookshop,
but at noon I'll be in the Gallery, the scent of black coffee,
a grain of sugar for bitter days, clean-shaven and brushed,
hurrying by, running after honours, sure,
there's no end to elbowing, neither at work nor in politics.
I glance at the watch, might still catch Podlogar
with lunch vouchers, though today I'll only have half a helping,
after all I've been sated with all the hearts shining in the letter box,
on pavements and wedged in the cracks of cobbled streets,
I may not have found the key to Your breasts (and your heart
lost there), but I'll venture something crazy
nevertheless: to catch a moment in the crowd, a girl's
eyes, a woman's juice, or should I flip, heads or tails
to make do until tomorrow when again I'll turn
the key and perhaps find the secret equation
to our irresistible attraction, and a new heart
will become the object of the modern world's frenzy – here,
amid the seeming wellbeing of the happy,
wrapping up their former, oh, fought and ended battles,
the heartbeat is like an almost imperceptible embrace that promises
not to unlock itself even on the other side of the door.

Translated by Ana Jelnikar

Taja Kramberger was born in Ljubljana in 1970 and spent her childhood in the port of Koper (Capodistria) near the Italian border. She graduated in history from the University of Ljubljana (where she also studied archaeology) and continued her studies in historical anthropology as a postgraduate at the Ljubljana Graduate School of Humanities.

Her first book of poems, *Marzipan*, appeared in 1997, since when a further three collections have been published: *The Sea says* in 1999; the German-language *Counter-current* in a collectors' edition in 2002; and in 2004, *Mobilizations*, in four languages. Her work has been translated into a number of European languages.

Taja Kramberger is currently Editor-in-chief of *Monitor ISH – Review of Humanities and Social Sciences* and also works as a literary translator from French, Italian, English and Spanish.

TAJA KRAMBERGER

MOBILIZACIJE

Moja draga Zorka, pesem je zate

I MOBILIZACIJA ZA PREŽIVETJE

Včasih je bil moj oče kakor cedra,
osamelec, vraščen na
vrtu svojega življenja.
In veje, začenjajoče se dva metra nad tlemi,
so bile kot pradavne zimzelene želje,
ki so hotele zatipati nebo, se
oprijeti stvarnih zvezd, a so
na svoji poti olesenele.
In smola, ki je, kapljajoč iz ran,
dišavila zemljo, je
bila mrzla in hrumeča Volga
na begu iz sibirskih step,
usmerjena na jug.

Moj oče: priložnostni svetilnik,
ogrnjen v temen, zapackan suknjič, vedno
za potezo šahovskega konja
oddaljen od nas, v diagonali
črnega tekača odmaknjen od sebe; ali
pomrznjena regratova lučka
brez stopinj pod odsotnimi stopali.

In edina svetloba, ki je mežikala
v tej burkasti in temni pokrajini,
je prihajala
od spodaj:
bila je strnjena v kvadratu mačjega očesa,
na moji torbici za malo šolo,
rdeči: z obutim mačkom na prednji strani,
ki je bingljala z njegove velike dlanene zanke
pred mojimi očmi kakor viseči semafor.
Obuti ali sezuti maček ?

Kje so tedaj bile diplome rokoborca,
kje pepel spričeval z odliko, vloženih v krušno peč?
Upanje, sežgano med hlebci kruha.
Davno tedaj, ko je tvoj oče,
obubožani želar, ki ga nisem
utegnila spoznati, svet je zapustil pred mojim prihodom,

MOBILIZATIONS

My dear Zorka, this poem is for you.

1 MOBILIZATION FOR SURVIVAL

At times my father was like a cedar,
solitary, rooted
in the garden of his life.
And his branches, emerging two metres above the ground
were like ancient evergreen desires,
wanting to feel the sky, to
cling onto real stars, but they lignified
on their way.
And the resin which dripped from the wounds,
perfuming the earth was
the cold and roaring Volga,
fleeing from the Siberian steppes,
diverted towards the South.

My father: an occasional beacon,
wrapped in a dark, soiled jacket, always
a chess knight move
away from us and a diagonal distance
of the black bishop from himself; or
a frostbitten crown of a dandelion
without footprints beneath the absent feet.

And the only light to be shimmering
in this farcical, dark landscape
came
from beneath:
it was compressed in the square of a reflector
on my red primary school
bag: with the puss-in-boots on the front,
the reflector dangling from
the fingers of his chunky palm like suspended traffic lights.
A puss with or without the boots?

Where were the diplomas of the wrestler then,
where the ashes of the school reports with distinction, put into the baker's oven?
Hope, burnt amid loaves of bread.
A long time ago, when your father,
an impoverished crofter I
never got to meet – he had left this world before my coming –

izpod vročih kokoši kradel
družinske obroke, sveža
jajca in jih menjal za tobak, da bi
s črnim tobačnim izstrelkom sline – kar je pri tebi
zbujalo spoštovanje –
ubil muho v letu in
je tvoja mati z velikimi plazovi pridig
visoko zametla vhod v sanje.

Dunaj – Beograd – Pančevo.
Kje vse je svetil tvoj železniški signal:
rdeča kapa vlakovodje? Kam je zrl pogled, ki je drvel
po tirih, po jeklenih traverzah v svet? Kje so
kretnice, kjer si preusmerjal vlake
na drugi tir, dokler
ni tebe življenje samo potegnilo nanj?
Ladendorf – Frättingsdorf – Wätzleinsdorf.

Vse, kar je bilo,
je izpuhtelo, še pred
prihodom telesa.

Potem vpoklic na rusko fronto:
radiotelegrafist brez svojega orožja,
namesto radijske postaje Telefunken
so ti v roke stisnili
mitraljez, Mg 42,

stas: visok
kosa: smedja
oči: plave

vržen v deželo prepredeno z jarki, v razklenjene
čeljusti podhranjene zemlje,
pogoltne, ki čaka
na obljubljeno dostavo,

nos: pravi
brkovi: brije
osobeni znaci: nema

poslan v topo ždenje ruskih močvirij in
divje tuljenje izruvanih brez.

stole family meals
from beneath the brooding chickens, fresh
eggs, trading them for tobacco, so
his black jet of saliva – which
inspired your respect –
could kill a fly in mid-air,
the entrance to dreams snowed in by your mother,
her great torrents of rebuke.

Vienna – Belgrade – Pančevo.
Where did your railway signal flash:
the red conductor's cap? What did your eyes take in, rushing
along the tracks, along the metal crossbeams of the world?Where are the
switches on which you diverted trains
onto other tracks, until
life itself pulled you along them?
Ladendorf – Frättingsdorf – Wätzleinsdorf.

Everything there
vanished even before
the coming of the body.

Then the call-up to the Russian front:
an operator without his weapons,
instead of the radio station Telefunken
they pressed a machine gun, Mg 42,
into your hands.

height: tall
hair: brown
eyes: blue

cast into a country, crisscrossed with trenches, into gaping
jaws of starving earth,
gluttonous, waiting on
its *Taja Kramberger*

nose: straight
moustache: shaved
distinguishing marks: none

sent to obtuse dormancy of Russian swamps and
the wild wailing of uprooted birches.

Potem, ukaz:
na konici fronte vkop prve bojne linije
na hribu pred *pasienis,*
litvansko nebo kot
tesna pokrovka, ki pritiska k dnu,
in potem,
med zrelim pšeničnim klasjem,
puzanje za življenjem in za dunajskim kolegom,
čigar ime, *Swoboda,* je polno upanja
štrlelo v prihodnost. *No man's land,*
no man's life
z belim robcem predaje na mitraljezu
po omrtvičenem trebuhu
proti ruski artileriji,
proti svobodi.

Dezerter, ki ni mogel ubijati in je
zato ubijal zrak, a ni sklatil ptice.
Ubežnik pred sabo,
pred smrtjo in pred življenjem,
večno na begu v tem zakletem
trikotniku preživetja.

Tehnika pozitivnega transferja
je preseči plato, je kasneje zabeležila
taista roka; tvoja, ki je
v ruskem ujetništvu za
študente medicine s skalpelom
razpirala prsni koš trupel,
obolelih za vodenico,
in jim kot redke sadeže podajala organe
v tej smrtni ekonomiji, da bi ohranila
obtok krvi in organe v svojem telesu
na pravem mestu.

Suh prepečenec pod jezikom in
večni okus *kapusta sup,*
na tleh anorgansko tkanje: preproga mrtvih teles, – 42°C,
tvoja živa meja, *ligustrum vulgare,* ki
še danes poganja in cveti:
kategorije zloma ali atributi življenja?

Then, the command:
On the tip of the front – on a hill just before *pasienis* –
entrench on the front firing line,
the Lithuanian sky like
a tight lid, pressing down hard,
and then
amid ripe wheat spikes,
crawling for your life and for your Viennese colleague,
whose name, *Swoboda*, jutted into the future,
full of hope. *No man's land,*
no man's life,
with a white handkerchief of surrender tied to the machine gun,
on his benumbed stomach
towards the Russian artillery,
towards freedom.

A deserter who could not kill and
therefore killed air, but did not strike a bird.
A fugitive from himself,
from death and from life,
forever on the run in a damned
triangle of survival.

The technique of positive transfer
is to overcome a plateau, was later noted
by that same hand: yours, which
dissected corpses' chests
afflicted with dropsy
for medical students in the Russian prison camp
and then handed out the organs
as though they were rare fruits
in that deadly economy of keeping
your blood in circulation and your organs
in place.

Stale bread under your tongue and
the eternal taste of *kapusta sup*,
on the floor the inorganic weaving: a carpet of dead bodies, – 42°C,
your hedgerow, *ligustrum vulgare*,
which sprouts and blossoms still today:
categories of breakdown or attributes of life?

In tvoja mati, triindevetdesetkrat obhajana,
na Bokalcah fanatično obdana z ruskimi klasiki in
Kristusovimi križi, mi je običajno v roko stisnila
kot sonce veliko pomarančo,
ki je ni mogla pojesti, ker zobje že
dolgo niso bili več podobni mlinskim kamnom.
Žareči sadeži, ki so se kot živahna ozvezdja,
kot pomnožena sonca v sivini izteka,
nabirali na okenskih policah, čakajoč
z zobmi oborožene obiskovalce.
Ki jih nisem mogla
pojesti, ker se mi je zdelo, da notri čaka smrt,
življenje brez soka. Kljubovalne, suhe oranže, ki
so jih sestre z nezadržno vztrajnostjo
dostavljale za malico. V domu, kjer
je komaj kakšna sled kisika
mogla prebiti zmedeno nasičenost urina.
Smrtni ples vonjav
v zaraščenih nosovih, potuhnjen
v zasedi na trdih blazinah
invalidskih vozičkov s hodnikov.
Odsotni vonj življenja, ki se je naselil
v otroških nosnicah in globoko na dnu
oskubljenih stoletnih glav. V prebivališču
volje, hladnejše od orožja,
močnejše od smrti.

Kot cedrin storž majhna, trmasta ženica:
mati te je postavila v vrsto pogubljenih,
v kolonado kljubovalnih.
Mati te je, s tisočerimi zgrešenimi napoji in napori,
mobilizirala za preživetje. Ne odlična spričevala,
ne rokoborba, ne gimnastika pri Sokolu.

Kot drevo brez debla,
v neki davni noči brez spanca,
je moj oče leta 1946 stal
na rodni zemlji.
Vrnjen,
toda kam, čemu in komu? In
daleč je bilo sonce in
daleč pokrajina,
ki bi ga podpirala.

And your mother, celebrated ninety-three times,
fanatically surrounded by Russian classics and
crucifixes in Bokalci would squeeze an orange
into my hand, the size of the sun,
which she couldn't eat, because her teeth
had long since stopped resembling millstones.
Glowing fruits which gathered like animated constellations,
like multiplied suns in the grey ending
on the window sills, waiting
for visitors armed with teeth.
Oranges I could not
eat, for I felt death lurking inside,
life without juice. Defiant, dry oranges which
sisters would deliver for a midday break
with relentless persistence. In a home where
hardly a trace of oxygen
could penetrate the muddled saturation of urine.
A deadly dance of smells
in hairy noses, deviously
waiting in ambush on the hard seats
of wheel chairs from the corridors.
The absent scent of life that settled
the child's nostrils and inhabited the very bottom of
those plucked centenarian heads. In an abode
of will, colder than arms,
more powerful than death.

A stubborn old girl, as small as a cedar cone:
mother had put you in the line of the lost,
in the column of the defiant.
With thousands awry potions and exertions
mother mobilized you for survival. Not your outstanding grades,
nor wrestling or gymnastics at the Sokol club.

Like a trunkless tree,
one distant sleepless night in 1946,
my father stood on his
motherland.
Returned,
but where, what for, and to whom? And
far was the sun and
far the landscape
to support him.

II Mobilizacija za življenje

Čudak, odpadnik, ateist, ki
si išče zavetje v agronomiji,
Goetheju in dresuri otrok. Ki
ga življenje premetava po minskem polju
kakor neosedlanega šahovskega konja. Ki
opisuje črko L: *Lehrling,* a ne uporablja
osnovnih prestav in nikdar ne zavira.
Ki z nogama v mrzli kadi, za
boljšo koncentracijo, prebira
Krmo prašičev in v botaničnih knjigah
upa na odkritje krova,
tal pod nogami, a ne najde
lapuhovega lista,
dovolj velikega, da bi prekril njegovo senco.

Ki je moji mami na prvi zmenek prinesel šopek
iz dveh kuhalnic in se takoj zatem odmaknil
na distanco 800 km. In je na polju spet,
osramočen in muhast,
obrnil smer tekača,
nazaj k vladajoči šahovski figuri;
tisti, ki se brez napora zmore gibati
v vseh smereh, včasih le s pogledom
brez premika, k
njej, ki v sebi skriva
poteze vseh ostalih in bdi nad njimi.

In jaz: rezultat družinskega glasovanja
februarja 1970; nihče ni dal veta in embrio
se je nemoteno razvijal vame,
da bi danes mirno mogla opazovati svojo pot,
sled, že daljšo od življenja in da bi
pred seboj mogla videti
tvoje življenje, veliko daljše od poti.

In tako je moj oče vame vlagal svoj
nedokončani herbarij,
da so se moje misli drenjale med
kupi knjig kot sploščene bilke,
dokler se ni, v prvi zbirki, vsa ta
vegetativna učenost razletela

II MOBILIZATION FOR LIFE

An eccentric, deserter and atheist,
seeking refuge in agronomy,
Goethe and the discipline of children. Whose life
tosses him to and fro on a mine field
like an unsaddled chess knight. Who depicts
the letter L: *Lehrling*, but makes no use
of the basic gears and never brakes.
Who reads *Pigs Fodder*, his feet in a cold bath – to
improve concentration –
and who hopes to discover a shelter in botanical books,
the ground beneath his feet,
but cannot find a coltsfoot leaf
big enough to cover his own shadow.

Who brought my mother on their first date a bouquet
of two ladles and then removed himself
to a distance of 800 km. Once on the field, he
changed the course of the bishop again,
directing him back towards the regal chess piece;
the one that can move painlessly
in all directions, at times simply with a glance
without a move, towards her
hiding within herself
the moves of all moves, watching over them.

And I: the outcome of a family vote
in February 1970; nobody imposed a veto and the embryo
freely grew into me,
so that today I can calmly look upon my path,
a trail, already longer than life, so I
can see your life
ahead of me, much longer than the path.

And so my father invested his
unfinished herbarium into me,
and my thoughts crammed between
the piles of books like flattened flowers
until, in my first collection,
all this vegetative erudition exploded

in so vse skrbno razporejene trave
lahko zopet zavzele
svoj nekdanji volumen.
In zdaj, pred menoj: prostrana
pustinja bilk, besed, voljnih in svežih,
ki se krči in širi na moj ukaz,
kakor vesolje. Kaj naj
z njimi počnem, tu,
v tem skrotovičenem prostoru,
mrzlokrvnem.
In zdaj pred očmi: prostrana
enolična pampa
navadnih bingeljcev, Vulpia myuros,
prekrita z zavistnim drstom
amfibij.

Tvoj dvofazni, izmenični tok
in 1200 strani vročičnih zapiskov,
deročih z močjo
hudourniškega vrelca. Sifonsko
breme, ki si ga nam, svojim otrokom,
odložil na ramena, kot
odloži vojna sebično svoja trupla
in krvavi spomin v
nepredirni kolobar mita in ga
zakoplje za prihodnje generacije
med liste zemeljske knjige, v veliki
neizdani *hardback*
brez korektur in
brez založnika.

Je bil Bog skrit med čičeriko,
med sončničnim semenjem in korenjem,
v ustih distrofičnih ujetnikov
na poti domov?

Je bil Bog skrit v gluhih bobničih pištol, ki
so jih gestapovci tiščali vate na Dunaju,
ko ste *pubeci* sipali
pesek med osi tračnih kompozicij?

and all the blades, precisely ordered,
could once again occupy
their former volume.
And now I am faced with an endless
wasteland of flowers, words, willing and fresh,
contracting and expanding at my order
like the universe. What am I
to do with it, here,
in this twisted place,
cold-blooded.
And now in front of my eyes: an endless
featurless pampa
of *common danglers*, *Vulpia myuros*,
covered with an envious spawn of
amphibia.

Your diphase, alternating current
and the 1200 pages of frenzied notes,
gushing forth with the magnitude
of a hurricane spout. A siphonic
burden you have laid on
your children's shoulders, the way
a war selfishly lays its bodies
and its bloodied memory into
an impenetrable mythical ring and
buries it for the future generations
amid the pages of an earthly book, a large
unpublished hardback
with no corrections and
no editor.

Was God hidden amid chick-peas,
sunflower seeds and carrots,
in the mouths of distrophic prisoners
on their way home?

Was God hidden in the deaf eardrums of rifles
the Gestapo prodded you with in Vienna,
when you *lads* were shoveling
sand inside the axes of the railroad composition?

Je bil Bog skrit v Jaroslavu, v taborišču
iz prve svetovne vojne, v zobeh podgan, ki
so skakale čez ujetnike in vanje
čudežno niso zagrizle?

Materin Bog ali tvoj Nebog?
Oboje najavljeno z
veliko začetnico,
oboje v stiski izpihnjeno v temo
brez odgovora,
oboje otrplo in nebogljeno
kot čepenje v zaprtem sodu
Mohojeve bolote.

Ne ruska fronta, ne lakota, ne vino,
ne študij, ne –

nothing matters but the quality
of the affection –
in the end – that has carved the trace in mind
dove sta memoria –

mojega očeta je za življenje
mobilizirala moja mama,
mila in stanovitna ljubezen,
imenovana
Zorka.

Was God hidden in Jaroslav, an internment camp
from World War I, between the teeth of rats,
that, skipping across prisoners, surprisingly did not bite?

Mother's God or your non-God?
Both announced
in capital letters,
both, in an hour of need, puffed into darkness
without an answer,
both numb and frail
as if crouching in an enclosed barrel
of *Mohojeva bolota.*

It was neither the Russian front nor hunger, nor wine,
nor was it your studies, no –

        nothing matters but the quality
of the affection –
in the end – that has carved the trace in mind
dove sta memoria –

it was my mother who mobilized
my father for life,
the gentle and unfaltering love
named Zorka.

Translated by Ana Jelnikar

HUNGARY

PHOTO: GÁBOR VAJDA

JÁNOS TÉREY was born in 1970. Poet, writer and literary translator, he has won many Hungarian literary awards, including the prestigious Attila József Prize.

His most important publications to date are *The Natural Arrogance* (1993), *Possessors' Aspect* (1997), *Termann's Traditions* (1997) and *Paulus* (2001).

JÁNOS TÉREY

BEHARANGOZÁS

Majd bolond leszek ott megtelepedni,
ahol a legnagyobb az ínség:
Pokoltornácán nem leszen lakásom.
Fiatal fővel ott legyek ügyeletes tiszt?
Felügyeljem a tájat, száraz,
konok hidegben? – Majd ha fagy.
Nem lehetne onnét eltávozásom.
Kóstolhatnám Pokoltornác tájborait.
Nem volna senkivel beszédem. Magamban
szidnám a lőrét, és füle volna a falnak.
Valaki gyomorszájon vágna, jaj,
váratlan, könyörtelen tettlegesség
– „tanulj tisztességet, szép öcsém!" –,
próbálnám hárítani a csapásokat
s levegőbe markolna puszta kezem.

Pokoltornácán ne legyen lakásom –
így fohászkodtam villanyoltás előtt.
Álmomban fölkeresett bátyám, Bezzeg úrfi.
Mellemen ugrált, háromszor szólított:

„Öreglegény, öreglegény! Ha tudnád,
mi minden voltam én a te korodban.
Ember és polgár, apa és civil.
Az élők sorában mosolyogva álltam.
Háznépem volt, úgy becéztem őket: az enyéim."

„Öreglegény, egyedül vagy, mint az ujjam.
Múltad rovott, s a legújabb rovátkád: dögrovás.
Kaptál időt a földön, kifutottál az időből.
Magad alatt vagy, fekszel pincemélyi zugban."

„Öreglegény, elveszejtelek. Megvonom
szádtól a falatot és elmédtől az álmot.
Az égadta világon nincs többé maradásod.
Fogod magad, Pokoltornácára költözöl,
majd ha fagy, majd ha bolond leszel.
Fagyott az éjjel, nem voltál az utcán
idefönt virrasztottál velem, jó bolond."

ANNOUNCEMENT

I'd be crazy to settle where
famine is the ruler:
I won't have my home on the Porch of Hell.
Should I, a young man, be the officer on duty over there?
To watch over the land in such a dry,
obstinate cold? – Only when the sun freezes.
I wouldn't be able to leave from there.
I'd be tasting the wine of the region of the Porch of Hell.
There'd be no one to talk to. I'd abuse
the bad wine myself, and the walls would have ears.
Someone would hit my stomach, ouch,
sudden, ruthless assault
– "learn decency, good brother!"–,
I'd try to ward off the blows
and my bare hands would grasp air.

Don't make me have my home on the Porch of Hell –
I prayed before the light turned dark.
In my dream I've got a visitor, my brother, Prince Sure Enough.
Jumping on my chest, he called me three times:

"Old boy, old boy! If you only knew
what I'd been at your age.
Man and bourgeois, father and civilian.
I stood among the living smiling.
I've got tenants, I've addressed them nicely: you're all mine."

"Old boy, you're alone, like my finger.
Previously convicted, and your newest conviction is pestilence.
You've got time, still you ran out.
You're beyond yourself lying in a basement-deep hollow."

"Old boy, I'll get rid of you. I'll take
the food out of your mouth and the dream out of your mind.
You won't stay on Earth any longer.
You'll get ready to move to the Porch of Hell,
only when the sun freezes, when you're crazy.
Last night it was freezing, you weren't out on the street,
you kept yourself awake with me, you righteous fool."

Fényesség van, nem látom bátyámat,
Bezzeg úrfit. Minden zaj ismerős, otthoni.
A halandó, aki fölébred, élni kénytelen.
Déli harang kondul, elszólít hazulról:
van haladékidőm és van sétaterem.

AZ IKREK GYÁSZBESZÉDE

Mert eldőlhettek délelőtt az Ikrek,
  S nem tart építményt elsöpört alap,
S egyetlen apparátuslakta szintet
  Sem rejt már tornyok méhe: térfogat –
Behódolt égbolt, pásztázhat tekintet,
  Hol Ikrek álltak, az a sáv szabad.
Borzolt bordáik úgy merednek égre,
Mint sárkánygyík vázának csonka kérge.

Megroppan, tőke tornya: torkametszett;
  Zúzott mellkassal dől a második;
Látom hulltát érinthetetleneknek,
  Kiket gőgjükben terror tántorít.
Üvegfüggöny szilánkjai peregnek,
  Látványul szolgál, táj ha változik;
S ha délelőtt az Ikrek összedőlnek:
Csak téboly magja, agyrémből előleg.

A Nulla Zóna: hely, leróni jókor
  Hóbortomért az elkésett adót –
Valósulandó vágyam a gonosztól
  Átrajzolt táj sakktábla-képe volt,
S a kihűlt kataklizma-városokból
  Ereklyét hoztam, kézzelfoghatót.
A tapasztalat tisztasága lep meg,
Hogy nincsenek végleges sziluettek.

It is bright now. I can no longer see my brother,
Prince Sure Enough. Every sound is familiar, homely.
When a mortal awakens, he is forced to live.
Midday bell tolls, takes me away from home:
I have time to spare and space to walk.

Translated by Michael Castro and Gabor G. Gyukics

FUNERAL ORATION FOR THE TWINS

Since both Twins had collapsed before high noon,
    And crushed foundations won't support a wall,
Nor will the tower-womb shelter even one
    Lost storey – phone-line, boardroom, terminal –
There's space in the conquered sky, the gaze may run
    Straight down two airwells marking the Twins' fall.
Their rattled ribs reach for the deepening dusk
Like a serpent skeleton's discarded husk.

The tower of capital cracks: its throat is slit;
    The second with a chest wound starts to slide.
I watch the untouchables falling, bit by bit,
    Rocked by sheer terror in their pomp and pride.
Glass-curtains cascade down, their slivers split;
    Once landscape changes, tourists need a guide.
And if one morning the Twins are just not there,
It's only a taster, the first seeds of despair.

Ground Zero is the place where I may clear
    Unsettled debts that fund my quirkiness –
My dream came true: the landscape should appear
    Wickedly redrawn: a board for chess,
Recalling relics of earlier sites of fear:
    Wrecks tangible in ordinariness.
What's shocking is the singularity:
No previous patterns fit reality.

(Eszembe jut majdnem-kasszandraságom,
    Játékom tűzzel, jós-önkívület:
Paulust ezüstfehér burokba zárom,
    Robbantva első betonikremet;
És torzó-szkeletont hagyok a tájon…)
    Ha rossz vért szült százszor modellezett
Manhattan-égés: be kellett tetézze
Szennyember szörnyebb elmeszüleménye.

Azé, aki csípőjénél fogva csapja
    Földhöz fantomját – égbe így kiált,
De épített országon sincs hatalma.
    Égszint, hatálya vesztett felvilág!
Hol jártam egykor: emberraj kutatja
    A holtak első elitcsapatát.
Credo quia absurdum. Bárki voltam
A látott, meg sem énekelt New Yorkban.

JÉZUS SZEGÉNYEI

Hideglelős, nappali nők! meg ti, akik
mint a zsinagóga macskái, úgy tüzeltek!
    nem duzzoghattok tovább fészketekben,
    egy profán férfi jön vizitre este.

Jó diagnosztának számítotok mind,
pedig fogalmatok sincs, ki küldte
    rátok a sikamlós pribéket,
    a vasárnap esti látogatót.

Gyakran csak lágy akarnok,
ezúttal azonban az erőtöket akarja.
    Viharkabátban férközik hozzátok,
    szezámmagot szemelgetve kivár.

Őrzőitek alszanak: most csap szét közöttetek.
Ragaszkodik a láthatáshoz, ősi vendégjogához,
    és elragad titeket kedveseitektől.

(Now I recall my near-Cassandra vein:
    Playing with fire, in vatic delirium,
I wrap up brother Paul in a silvery skein
    And blow my concrete twin to kingdom come
Leaving a skeleton, a twisted frame...)
    Burning Manhattan models for the sum
Of all bad-blood; it is the climax where
The worst can realize their bleak nightmare.

He who grabs his opponent by the hip
    And floors him, cries out to the heavenly host
But lacks power to wreck human workmanship.
    Heaven is a region where such power is lost.
The streets that I walked men rake over and strip
    To seek the dead elite, first at their post.
Credo quia absurdum. Wherever I now belong
I saw New York but left the town unsung.

Translated by George Szirtes

THE POOR PEOPLE OF JESUS

You shivery women of the day! and you who
rut like the synagogue's cats!
    you can't sulk any more in your cosy nests,
    a profane man comes for a visit in the evening.

You all seem to be good detectives,
though you don't have a clue who sent you
    this slippery hangman
    this Sunday evening visitor.

Often he is only a soft social climber,
this time however he's after your strength.
    He approaches you in a trench-coat,
    and hangs around, selecting sesame seeds.

Your guards are sleeping: now he pounces on you all.
he insists on being seen, on his ancient right of hospitality,
    and takes you from your lovers.

(Rossz évszak, langyos botránykrónikák
az összes megzizzenő estilapban.)

Ki celebrál misét közületek a fiatalúrért,
ezért a jenkiért, aki daccal lép elétek
és önkezéről esik hamar el?

LITÁNIA: A JÓ LÁNY

A jó lány a huzatban ébred,
vizet paskol magára és szolgálni kész.
A jó lány szerepel a köztudatban,
tüzet kér tőlem, aztán nincs nyoma.
A jó lány kíváncsi a mondakörre,
mely mindőnket méltatlanul övez.
Szorgoskodik, hogy föltaláljon, földerítsen,
a jó lány nem bocsájtja meg a múltam.
Szemem láttára öltözik a jó lány,
hogy lássam, nem szeplőtelen egészen.
Ő sokkal hasznosabb, mint gondolom;
otthonosan mozog számos vidéken,
utazni visz, utaztatja a nyomorunkat,
úgy köp, mint én, minden vacak tavaszra.

(Bad season, lukewarm chronicles of scandals
  in every rustling evening paper.)

Who, from among you, will celebrate a mass for the young man,
for this Yankee, who stepped in front of you obnoxiously
  and soon will fall by his own hand?

LITANY: THE GOOD GIRL

  The good girl awakens in a draft,
splashes water on herself, and is ready to serve.
The good girl's roles are all common knowledge,
she asks for a light, then disappears.
The good girl is interested in all the surrounding legends
we don't deserve.
She is zealous to invent, to discover,
the good girl doesn't forgive me my past.
The good girl gets dressed in front of me
so I can see that she is not at all spotless.
She is more useful than I think:
she's at home in every neighbourhood,
she takes me along on trips, exercising our misery,
she spits the same way I do, at every trashy spring.

Translated by Michael Castro and Gabor G. Gyukics

PHOTO: ISTVÁN FAZEKAS

KRISZTINA TÓTH is one of Hungary's most highly acclaimed young poets. Winner of several awards, including the Graves Prize (1996), the Déry Tibor Prize (1996) and the József Attila Prize (2000), her poetry has been translated into many languages.

Her poems have strong connections with different Hungarian and European poetic traditions (she translates French poetry), their trademark being a subtle combination of strong visual elements, intellectual reflection and a very empathic, yet often ironic, concern with everyday scenes, conflicts and people.

Krisztina Tóth lives in Budapest where, apart from writing and translating poetry, she designs and produces stained glass windows.

KRISZTINA TÓTH

KÜLD EGY MOSOLYT

I

Múltkor a metrón egy idegen arcban a szemedbe néztem.
Vannak ilyen napok amikor minden úgy emlékeztet.
Valaki valakire leszállsz elébekerülsz mégsem.
De ez egy másik év ami múlt folyton nem létezhet.

Egy régi osztálytársam is szembejött ugyanúgy még gyerekként.
Különben sose hittem el hogy mi is egyszer.
Istenem mennyire mennyire szerettem volna melléd.
Ott állsz a metrón és puff egyszercsak megöregszel.

Szoktam gondolni rá mit szólna egymáshoz ez a két test.
Hogy milyen lehet az illatod biztos ma már más.
Hogy vajon tudna-e szólni egymáshoz ez a két test.
Ahol a kisfiam született van egy vékonyka vágás.

Valahogy szélesedik a csípőm is nem tudom mire vélni.
Ezt az egészet nem boldogít igazán nem is fáraszt.
Különös volt abba a másik arcba belenézni.
Idegen szemeiddel láttad ugye idegen számat.

II

Néha megijedek ha megszólalok meghallom az anyámat.
Múltkor a moziban a tükörből szinte rám szólt.
Ahogy a szappant fogta hirtelen az az érzésem támadt.
Mire volt jó az a sok szaros év hogy kár volt.

Sőt a férfi akivel élek vele is bizonyos hangsúlyokban.
Meg a kutyánk főleg a nézésében de tényleg.
Az anyámmal az előbb különben nem túloztam.
De látod nem is tudom ezekről mért beszélek.

Utolsó karácsonyom volt gyerekként kaptam egy macskát.
Egy közért mellett laktunk hó volt forgalmas úton.
Meglátott futott elém akkor szaladt át.
Hányadszor kéne annyi mindent megtanulnom.

SEND A SMILE

I

The other day I looked into your eyes in a stranger's face on the metro.
There are these days when everything somehow jogs my memory.
Someone's a bit like someone you get off look at them and then no.
But this is another year past things can't be never-ending.

In the same way an old classmate walked towards me just as she
         was in childhood.
I never thought it would happen to us too incidentally.
Oh god how much I would have liked to be beside you.
You're standing there in the metro and bang you grow old suddenly.

I often wonder how they'd react to each other these two bodies.
What your smell would be like I'm sure it must be different now.
If they even could react to each other these two bodies.
There's a thin scar where I gave birth to my son.

Somehow my hips are getting wider as well I don't know the reason.
For all this I find nothing really either pleases or tires out.
Looking into that other face was so confusing.
There you were with your stranger's eyes looking at my stranger's mouth.

II

Sometimes I get frightened I seem to hear my mother when I'm speaking.
At the cinema recently she almost talked to me from a mirror.
The way she held the soap suddenly I was struck by the feeling.
All those shitty years what a pointless waste they were.

Not to mention the man I live with in certain familiar intonations.
Our dog also reminds me a lot when it looks at me that way.
About my mother just now I wasn't exaggerating.
Mind you why I'm talking about all this stuff I can't say.

It was the last Christmas when I was still a child I got a kitten.
We lived next to a food store the busy road was snow-covered.
It saw me ran to me crossed the road in that instant.
How many times over must I learn these things.

Mielőtt akár egy kavics gesztenye egy falevél is.
Azt válaszolnád éppen ezért és lehet ebben.
Valami hogy én aki láttam és tudom én is.
Hülyeség mondom a teremtés strébere lettem.

III

Tavaly ősz elején amikor beköltöztünk ebbe a házba.
Minden csupa higító festék meg csupa por volt.
Vártuk megváltozik a szag a lélegzetünktől hátha.
Aztán egyre hűvösödött nem is emlékszem hogy volt.

Egyszercsak nem lehetett már reggelenként a teraszra.
Kiültél vitted a kávét és fázni kezdtél kabát.
Nélkül nélkül az üres helyeket hogy belakja.
Valahogy elrendezi ez ember feltalálja magát.

Olyan furcsa ez a mai fény mint egy távoli évszak.
Mintha valaki más lennék vagy inkább valahol máshol.
Be is mentem egy kardigánért hiába még csak.
Nem is színekből inkább a levegő állagából.

Tudni nem a nyár rajzolódik ez az ősz arca.
Szájforma rozsdafolt hallgat nézd a levélen.
Bámul a kisfiam régről csecsemőszemű macska.
Szélcsend vékony füstjele nézem nézem.

BUDAPESTI ÁRNYÉKOK (ÁLOM, FOTÓ, MORAJ)

Köves Éva: Budapesti árnyékok (vászon, fotó, olaj)

I

A hold neonja hullik,
kilobbant ég a hóra.
Átfordul, visszaperceg.
Ébrenlét, homlokóra.

Prior to let's say a pebble a chestnut a tree leaf.
You'd answer that's exactly why and actually it could be.
A thing that I know as well and who'd seen it.
Nonsense I say I've become creation's keenest student.

III

Last year at the beginning of autumn when we first moved into this house.
Nothing but dust paint everywhere nothing but paint thinner.
We hoped perhaps our breathing would change it chase the whiff out.
Then it got gradually cooler after that I can't remember.

Suddenly in the mornings we couldn't go out on the terrace.
You sat with a coffee and started to get cold with your coat.
Off with your coat off try to settle in the empty places.
Somehow you sort things out you manage to fall on your feet.

Like some far-off season this light of today it's so unhomely.
It's as if I'm somebody else or more like I'm elsewhere.
I went inside for a cardigan even though it's still only.
Not so much the colours it's more the quality of today's air.

To know it's not summer sketching itself but the face of autumn.
See that leaf a mouth-shaped rust patch silently stains it.
My little son stares from the past a baby-eyed kitten.
Still air's thin smoke signal I gaze at gaze at.

Translated by David Hill

SHADOWS OF BUDAPEST (DREAMS, PHOTOS, ROARS)

Éva Köves: Shadows of Budapest (canvas, photos, oils)

I

The moon's neon light falls,
a flare of sky in the snow.
Turning, ticking, switching back.
Wakefulness, brow of the hour.

II

Menni a hídon, át Budára.
Nem is folyó meg nem is álom,
vízben vándorló vastraverszek.
Sietek, mert én vagyok a lakásom.

III

És megy az utca negatívján
Ahonnan jött, mindig csak arra.
Benyit háttal, hiába kongat
Az emlékezet térharangja.

IV

Hogyha befelé hazaérne,
Sötétből vissza a sötétbe,
Világos volna: egy velem.
Létezhetnék, *kétségtelen*.

V

Véletlen fénye ír a karján
Fekete csíkot. Odaállt,
Állna tovább, de megy a csík is.
Marad: *tétova tetovált.*

VI

Homályos perc, próbálok kitalálni.
Próbálok valamit, hogy kitaláljak.
Ha volna szál. Aki kezembe adná.
Egy szál gyufám. Ha volna Ariadné.

VII

Itt kéne hagyni az Egészet,
aogyan belőlem kiváltál,
részetlen részem. Úgy teszek
mindent, úgy élek, mintha látnál.

II

Crossing the bridge to Buda.
Neither river nor yet dream,
iron girders traverse the water.
I hurry, for I am my home to me.

III

Along the negative of the street,
coming from there, always thence.
Entering back first, despite the toll
of memory's bells in space.

IV

Were he to come home, inward,
from the dark back into the dark,
it would be clear: he's at one with me.
I could then be *unquestioningly.*

V

Chance light on his arm inscribes
a stripe of black. There he stands
and would go but so would the stripe.
He stays: *tattooed in two minds.*

VI

An obscured moment, I try to find an exit.
I try something in order to exit.
If there were a thread. Someone to proffer it.
If I had a single match. If there were Ariadne.

VII

I ought just to leave the Whole Thing,
as you bodied forth from me,
a part of me that is not. What I do,
everything, is to live as if you were watching.

VIII

Számtalan részlet elhagyódik.
Hol teste, hol csak arca van.
Húzódik bent egy végtelen híd,
visszhangtalan, *visz hangtalan*.

IX

És egyenesen oda fut ki,
névtelen utcán visz az álmod.
Fehérből feketébe lépked.
Sietek, mert én vagyok a lakásod.

X

Néz lefelé a lassú vízbe:
Milyen máélységes mély a nemrég.
Holdlátta csend, semmit se tükröz.
Mióta folyik ez a képtelenség

VIII

Countless detail gets discarded.
Only nightfall or a face remains.
An endless bridge extends within,
no echo barks, *noiseless it arcs.*

IX

And it leads straight there, your dream
sweeps you along a street with no name,
crossing from white into black and back
I hurry, for I am your home to you.

X

Looking down into the waters so slow:
how deep the deep of this 'not long ago'.
Moonstruck silence mirroring none.
How long has all this been flowing on.

Translated by Peter Sherwood

ROMANIA

PHOTO: GHEORGHE ERIZANU

Emilian Galaicu-Păun was born in 1964 in Unchitesi, Moldova and received a doctorate from the Maxim Gorky Institute of Literature in Moscow in 1989. He is Bessarabian Editor of *Vatra* and Editor-in-chief of the publisher Editura Cartier. He has published six collections of poetry, prose, translations and an essay, *The Poetry after Poetry* (Editura Cartier, Chisinau, 1999).

EMILIAN GALAICU-PĂUN

POEMA CONCEPȚIEI IMACULATE

nepereche în nopțile cînd își desface picioarele, unul mai fără-
nceput
și sfîrșit decît altul, ca două războaie
mondiale – înscriși între ele, cei douăze's'unu de ani ai lui, cînd *a
intrat la ea*, de perioadă
interbelică, taie măsura exactă a pasului, linia coapsei, *măiastra* de
aer a golului dintre
craci, cum ai șlefui cu germana lui *das ewig weibliche* pronunția
franțuzească (*chercher la femme*) – și care-i vor fi inspirat
comparația grație semnului
din născare în formă de tanc, de pe latura interioară a gambei, cu
țeava-ndreptată în sus, țintind sexul
(o poveste a gestului: mîna adusă la burtă a tinerei
profesoare de mate, în chiar timpul lecției cînd, despicîndu-l în două,
o coloană de tancuri sovietice tocmai intra-n sat, ca pentru a-și
feri sarcinat fătul zvîcnind prima oară-n turela maternă de *cha(i)r*
la atingerea
celei care, la tablă, cu creta-ntre dește – ea însăși ca dată cu var –
explica: "două linii paralele
nu se intersec...")

fată mare, înjură de *nașterea mă-si/*
se roagă de *doamne,*
maica domnului. numele ei fie tanka, chiar dacă-i maria. în numele
precistei poartă cu grație
cele două războaie – cel stîng, cu *war*ice! – prin inima tîrgului,
nepăsătoare la trecerea timpului – zebră de
zile albe și negre –, la focul pieziș din privirea bărbaților – mama
zicea: "de pisică
și de om te desparți la intrare, altminteri nu scapi de ei" –, cum ai
străbate un
cîmp minat fără hartă, închisă în propria sa carapace – tanchistă din
naștere – ca o zeiță-n armură. blin-
dată-n *nașterea mă-si!* ușoară de parcă nici maică-sa n-a fost în
veci grea cu dînsa,
nici fecioara maria cu Unul născut nu făcut (o poveste de dragoste:
cum s-au luat
golul dintre picioare cu goala stăpînă-a acestora, -n sensul că *cine
s-aseamănă
se adună*).
istoria trece cu pas de femeie: în '89, pe 7 noiembrie,
-n timpul paradei
militare, culcată sub tancuri, alături de alte o sută, luată-n

THE POEM OF THE IMMACULATE CONCEPTION

singularly alone in the night when she spreads open her legs, one no
    more without beginning and end than the other, like two world
wars – transcribed between them those twenty-one years of him
    when *he entered her*, the interwar
period, cutting the precise measure of her gait, the line of the thigh,
    the *bird in space* of air in the emptiness between
the legs, as, with a German *das ewig weibliche*, his French pronunciation
gets polished (*chercher la femme*) – a comparison which will be of
    inspiration to him owing to the birthmark
in the form of a tank along the flesh inside her thigh, its barrel pointed
    straight up, aiming at her sex
(a story of gesture: a hand applied to the belly of the young
maths teacher exactly at lesson time when, dividing it in two,
a column of Soviet tanks had entered the village, so as to safeguard
    her pregnancy
                the foetus in the maternal turret twitching
    for the first time at her touch,
she who, at the blackboard, a stick of chalk between her fingers –
    herself as if coated with lime – explains: "two parallel
lines never intersect…")

    in her maidenhood, the girl curses *Damn my mama's birth*
                    prays *O Lord,*
Mother of God. she lets her name be Tanka even though it's Mary.
    in the name of The Holy Virgin, she wears the two
wars – the left with the *war*icose vein! – through the very heart of
    town, graceful and indifferent to time's passing – zebra crossing of
white days and black – under the oblique fire of men's glances – my
    mama always said, "from cat
and man you must separate yourself upon your entrance, otherwise
    you can't escape either"– as if crossing
a minefield without a map, closed within her own shell – tank-woman
    from birth – like a goddess robed in armour. iron-
clad by her mama's birth! carelessly as if her mother had never
    been pregnant with her nor
the Virgin Mary with the One born but not conceived (a story of
    love: how the emptiness
between his legs took as wife her emptiness, mistress of all, in the
    sense that *like*
attracts like).
            history proceeds with a woman's gait; in '89, on the
    7th of November during
the military parade, is bedded beneath the tanks beside the hundred

căruță de
ofiţerul ulise ieşind din cei (cîţi?) cai-putere pîn' la epoleţi: "ăsta
   calcă, nu f…!";
ridicată-n picioare în '91, o dată cu statul, golem scrisţfăcut cu
degetul în ţărînă, să-i vină doar numele "r(î)m(a)"; să nu i se vadă
semnul fiarei? *wari*cele? de pe picioare, cu cizmele de cernoziom
   trase pînă
peste ochi (*Requiescat in pace!*); pe drumuri (nici unul nu duce
   la roma
decît *via* albania!)-n ultimii ani; adunată
cu genunchii la gură, cum şi-ar legăna, abia rupţi de la ţîţă, doi
   gemeni.
în puterea ei – facerea; mîinilor lui nu-i s-a dat decît scrierea.
şi atunci numai după ce-i intră sub piele, se face în tancul
de pe latura interioară a gambei, aprinde motoarele, pune-n
mişcare pistoanele, trage
ţintind sexul
                 (poema concepţiei imaculate se rupe
de pe buze: "desfă-mă!")

„$V_{A}{}^{C}A$~"

tatăl nostru cel carele-n cer eşti pripon precum eu pe pămînt
                 îţi sînt vaca legată cu funia *mu*

   II

care funie e predicat fiindcă: 1) arată ce face subiectul şi 2) că
   răspunde la
întrebarea *ce face?* familia şcoala m-au
învăţat că suniect este „vaca": ea smulge –
diateză activă – priponul. de mic *vac*cinatu-m-au anti-
dumnezeu: pentru mine priponul l-a smuls
tatăl meu pămîntesc păpuşarul l-a dat la kier vechi a pus mîna
   pe funie
şi m-a dus bou la şcoală să-nvăt
împreună cu alţi papă-lapte a-mi pune
întrebarea al cărei răspuns îl conosc, cît pe ce să

others taken in the carriage
of Officer Ulysses spending himself according to his (how many?)
    horsepower up to his epaulettes: "This man treads lightly, not f…!";
is raised upright in '91 at the same time as the state, a golem inscribed
                traced with
a finger in the dust, fitted solely for the name "worm"; so as not to see
the mark of the beast? the *warts*? on legs, black earth clinging
    to boots drawn up
over the eyes (*Requiescat in pace!*) and on the roads in recent
    years; is in-gathered
with knees drawn up to the mouth, as if rocking a pair of twins just
    torn away from her nipples.
in her power: conception. only writing has been granted for his
    handiwork.
and then, after he enters under her skin, it comes about that, in the tank
along the inside of her thigh, the engines start, the pistons thrust, he
    shoots,
aiming at her sex
           (the poem of the immaculate conception tears itself
from the lips: "open me!")

"V_{AC}C_A~ "

Our Father who art in heaven you are the iron stake as I on earth am
            the cow tethered to you by the rope *moo*

    II

which rope is a predicate because: 1) it shows what the subject is
    doing and 2) it answers
the question *what's going on*? the family school taught me
that the subject is "cow": it pulls out –
the active voice – the stake. as a child they *cow*ed me by *vacci*nating
    me anti-
God: for me they pulled out the stake
my earthly father the puppeteer brought it to the junkyard he took
    me by the rope
and led me to school like an ox on a lead to learn
together with other milksops and mooncalves to ask
the question I knew the answer to. I was on the point of
coming back like a cow. oh innocence lost together with the

mă-ntorc vacă. ah tu inocenţă pierdută odată cu primul de
    „ce-s?“
şi ca unui copil ce-şi surprinde părinţii
făcînd dragoste astfel mi s-a-nfăţişat adevărul. Îl recunoscui:voi *mu-*
ri! a fost ca şi cum mă născusem din nou: m-am smuncit din
aşternut rămînînd nemişcat. numai funia *mu*
a vibrat şi vibraţia ei a-mplut aerul de
circumvoluţiuni „nu-i-lumină
nicări...“ tot de-atunci eu am cearcăe. gata oricînd
să-mi înnod funia *mu* – diateză
reflexivă – în jurul grumazului. de la un timp e doar noduri
    cercînd să-i
dau de capă prin mîini mi-a trecut
ca un şir de mătănii: de nenumărate ori una şi-aceeaşi „de ce-s?“
    şi „de ce-s?“
pîn cuvintele s-au contopit între ele. cîndva – diateză pasivă –
funia *mu* mă va duce la el. care stăa şi înghite
în sec noduri la fel cum din versul-poem
Tibi vero gratias agam quo clamore? amore morer ore re
eu înghit cîte-o literă pînă-mi stă-n gît *ore re-*

III

alitatea: cu patru picioare cu uger cu coarne cu coadă în vîrful
căreia ghilimelele sînt pămătuf. *find băiet* de la coada
vacii n-am fost trimis niciodată cu vaca – relaţia cu
patrupedul fiind stabilită prin asociaţie: puşti
cînd făceam cîte-o poznă bunica-mi striga
„faraonule“! carnea mea – şapte cavi albe cu lapte mîncate de
    şapte vaci negre şi sterpe – de-actunci e-un
vis de groază din care trezindu-mă – să-l
tălmăcească – trimit după preot. şi preotul după
clpotar. şi el după gropar. la comanda „hei-rup!“ ei smulg robul
din celula de temniţă (bine'nţeles că
harbar n-au de ce-a zis anton pavlovici: „zilnic
să-ţi storci robul din tine“) şi-n grabă mi-l înfăţişează. cuvintele lui
mi le bag ca pe un stetoscop în urechi:

first "why is it?"
and as to a child who surprised his parents
making love so truth showed itself to me. I recognized it: I must *moo-*
ve on to the next world! it was as if I'd been born again: I tugged on
my bedsheets though I remained motionless. only the rope *moo*
vibrated and its vibration filled the air with
circumvolutions. "there's no light
anywhere…" since then I've had dark circles under my eyes always
ready
to tie myself to the rope *moo* – the reflexive
voice – around my neck. for a long time since then it's been only
    knots. as I tried to
get to its point it passed through my hands
like a string of rosary beads: a lot of the time merely "why is it?"
    and again the same "why?"
until the words perhaps are melted together – the passive voice –
by the rope *moo* I will be led to him. like he who stays and wants to
swallow the moon as in that poem in verses
Tibi vero gratias agam quo clamore? Amore more ore re
I swallow a letter until it sticks in my throat *ore re-*

III

ality: with four legs an udder horns a tail on the tip of which
quotation marks make a whiskbroom. oh, when I was a wee lad
following along at the cow's tail
never was I sent to tend the cow – my relation with
the quadruped being established by this association: as a little kid
when I played a prank my grandmother yelled at me
"you pharaoh!" my flesh – seven white cows fat with milk eaten up
    by seven black and ill favoured cows – since then
it's a frightful nightmare from which I wake up – to interpret
it – and send for the priest. and the priest sends for
the bell ringer. and he sends for the gravedigger. at the command
"one two three up!" they pick
the slave right out of his prison cell (it goes without saying
they didn't have a clue about what anton pavlovich said: "everyday
you have to squeeze the slave out of you") and they hurriedly present
    him to me. his words
strike my ears as through a stethoscope:

IV

„un poem este – aidoma unui imperiu. cum este
un imperiu? aidoma unui stomac de bovină – cîntaţi
împreună cu noi *vaca paşte
iarbă verde...* – cu două cămări: cea mai mare-i ca
    o magazie
unde iarba se culcă-n cămaşa ei verde şi noaptea
se trezeşte în zeghe vărgată-n cămara
cea mai mică, dar care de fapt întreţine digestia («nu te
întrista, a spus tata, pleci dintr-o
închisoare mai largă într-una mai strîmtă») eu am
ridicat o cincime din ţară – cîntaţi
împreună cu noi *floicele
pe cîmpii...* – şi-am închis-o-n cămara mai mică. am pus
străji de jur împrejur. am pus zgardă curentu-
lui electric şi botniţa i-am aruncat-o cît colo. l-am tot asmuţat şi
i-am dat drumul pe sîrma ghimpată şi («... iar
la ieşire nu te bucura, a mai spus, vei schimba doar
o-nchisoare mai strîmtă pe una mai largă») astfel am
împărţit şi am împaărăţit. repetaţi
împreună cu noi: un poem
este – aidoma unui imperiu: el are stomac
de bovină: abia după ce-a îghiţit la cuvinte începe
să le mistuie: laptele lui
noi *îl bem cînd e seara îl bem la amiaz dimineaţa îl bem şi la
    noapte îl bem
şi îl bem.* subsemnat: iosif vis-

V

sarionovici şi fraţii săi". un vers lat un vers fără de capăt precum
    paralela
de 66° 33' latitudine Nord înconjoară poemul de jur împrejur.
peste cercul polar al gîndirii am fost deportaţi noi supuşii cu sînge
cald ai inimii unde din ceruri coboară pe mii de
funii *mu* transcendenţa în chip de ninsoare şi spînzură
ca i naruibetă-n văzduh unde spaţiul
este una cu timpul: pustie scoţîndu-şi pe cap aurora
borea;ă o *cămaşă pierdută la zaruni.* de-aici

IV

"a poem is – exactly the same as an empire. what is
an empire? exactly the same as the stomach of a bovine – sing
along with us *the cow grazes*
the grass so green… – with two larders: the bigger one is like
    a storehouse
where grass lies down in its green nightshirt and night
wakes up in coarse striped twill in the little
larder, which in fact sustains digestion. ('don't
be sad,' father said, 'you're leaving
a larger prison for a narrower one') I built
a fifth of the country – sing
along with us *the flowers*
flourish in the fields… – and I locked it up in the little larder. we put
guards all around. we put on a dog collar of
electricity and I threw the muzzle away. I sicced it on and
I set it loose at the barbed wire and ('…but
you won't be happy when you get out,' he went on saying, 'you'll
    just change
a narrower prison for a larger one') in this way
we handed out handouts and we had the upper hand. repeat
along with us: a poem
is – exactly the same as an empire. it has the stomach
of a bovine: hardly has it swallowed words when it starts
to digest them: its milk
we *drink in the evening we drink it at noon in the morning*
    we drink it and at night we drink it
and we drink it. signed: iosif vis-

V

sarionovich and his brothers." an expansive poetry an endless
    poetry just like
latitude 66° 33' North the poem goes round and round.
we have been deported beyond the arctic circle of thought we
    subjects with warm
blood in our hearts where transcendence descends from the sky
    along thousands
of rope *moos* in the likeness of snow and it hangs
like a marionette in the heavens where space
makes one with time: wildly stripping off the aurora
borealis as if a *shirt for which they did cast lots.* from this

ne există scăpare. doar dacă scriind un vers lat un vers fără de
    capăt precum
paralela de 66° 33' latitudine Nord te
laşi convins de cuvinte să fugi împreună cu ele. o
    „*vaca*" – o
poezi.

    VI

      „a recita
poezii în temniţă, încheie ion mureşan, este echivalent cu a organiza o
evadare în masă". serbăm, mureşan cristofor subsemnatul
    – trei crai de la
răsărit – aiua lui eminescu la gherla, într-unul din apetele
celularului mare „în formă d U foarte lat" – nu-i nevoie să
ridicaţi în sus mîinle să le agitaţi: „eminesc-U-U-U!" – într-una
din celule făcută urgent „casă mare" – cirtate din
eminescu (ţarţamurile de prosoape deschid şu îchid precum nişte
ghilimele fiecare citat) decorează pereţii alături de harta
româniei mari şi de „extrase din regulamentul intern" – împreună
cu o mie de tineri în zeghe vărgate – ah părul lor scurt
şi sîrmos ca gazonul englez pare-a fi tuns la zero de cel puţin zece
generaţii la rînd – numai ochi şi urechi, prin dorinţa de *libi*
vulnerabili. trag aer de gherla în piept — spaţul nu e decît diafragma
între timpul prezent şi trecut – şi expir bioxid de carbon de gulag:
„osip mandelstam # se povesteşte # in cele vreo cîteva luni
de detenţie # îngreţoşat de mizerie # în nu s-a atins niciodată
de mîncarea cazonă # era un poet deosebit de subţire # c-unsimţ
    înnăscut al
igienei # curat un schelet # peste umărul stîng aruncîndu-şi
toga cărnii # un publius ovidius naso-al gulagului # să-şi
ţină sufletul # le recita
delincvenţilor de drept comun # kilometri întegri de poeme # drept
    care-l
răsplăteau # mai ceva ca-ntr-o proză de borges # regeşte # o hrincă de
pîine albă pe zi". poezie, ah *panem et cirenses.*

no escape exists. only writing an expansive poetry an endless
    poetry just like
latitude 66° 33' North you
let yourself be convinced by the words to run away with them. a
    "*cow*" – a
poem.

VI

    "to recite
poems in prison," ion mureşan points out, "is the equivalent of organizing
a mass escape." we celebrate, mureşan cristofor and yours truly
    – we three kings of
Orient – on the eminescu anniversary at gherla, in one end
of the huge prison "in the shape of a broad U"– there's no need for us
to wave our hands above us and thus pay homage: "eminesc-U-U-
    U!" like at a rally – in one
of the cells suddenly transformed to "the big house"– quotations
from eminescu decorate the walls (a heap of towels open
and close each quotation like quotation marks) beside a map
of greater romania and "excerpts from the statutes of
    internment" together
with a thousand young people in coarse striped twill – oh their short
bristly hair like an english greensward cut to zero for at least ten
generations in a row – only eyes and ears, through the desire for
    elusive freedom –
libi. I inhale gherla air deep into my chest – not even the thickness
of my diaphragm between present and past – and I exhale the
carbon dioxide of the gulag:
"osip mandelstam # the story is told # in those months
of detention # disgusted by dirt and misery # never ate
mess-hall grub # he was an unusually delicate poet # with an
    innate sense of
hygiene # a pure skeleton # flinging over his left shoulder
the toga of flesh # publius ovidius naso of the gulag # to
sustain his breath # he'd recite
to the common criminals # whole kilometers of poems # whereupon
they rewarded him # better than in borges's prose # royally #
    with a portion
of white bread every day." oh poetry, *panem et circenses*.

VII

„oameni tare cuminţi. din popor. din poporul cu frica de
dumnezeu". parcă-am fi toţi de-o mamă. de parcă
ne-a făcut mama-n noaptea în care
vaca neagră-a-fătat o viţea şi viţeaua fatată-a faţato o viţea şi
viţeaua fătată
a fătat o viţea de la care – întorşi de la ţîţă – am supt.

VII

"a very docile population. the common people. a nation with fear of
god." as if we all were born to one mother. as if
the mother gave birth to us one night in which
*the black cow calved a heifer and the newly-calved heifer
    calved a heifer and*
that heifer calved a heifer from which – turned away from
    the tit – we sucked.

Translated by Adam J. Sorkin and Cristina Cîrstea

PHOTO: GERHARD CSEJKA

IOANA NICOLAIE was born in 1974 in Transylvania and studied Philology at the University of Bucharest. She has published three collections of poetry – *Photograph Not Retouched* (2000), *The North* (2002) and *Faith* (2003) – and been anthologised, with other younger poets, in *Windows* (1998), *40238 Tescani* (1999) and, in a review of contemporary Romanian poetry, in *Poésie* (Maison de la Poésie / Théatre Molière, Paris, 2003).

IOANA NICOLAIE

MULAJ

Se poate să fi fost celtă
cîndva scormonind după miezul roşu al munţilor
în portmonee înflorite drămuind
galeriile surpate
zîmbetul larg al rîului
ca o lamă de bărbierit tăind Valea Anieşului
Cormaia şi Ilvele

se poate vicleşugul băuturilor tari
al miedului închegat în canistre
să-mi fi decolorat părul
să-mi fi spălăcit genele
        şi pielea ca mozaicul

neputincioasele braţe să mi le fi amorţit
cu plantele agăţătoare vălurind
                peste bîrne

se poate depărtările
ca pietrele de moară să mă strîngă
în laringele opărit al cascadei
printre roţile de lemn mîncate
de arama nisipului şi lîna dărăcită

aurul şi plumbul
haitele de lupi coborînd tot mai des
se poate
şi mistreţii grohăind lîngă prispe
în negura celui mai greu urcuş
din dimineţile divizate sub neschimbatul şpalt

se poate să fi fost celtă
pomeţii mei laţi se suprapun peste alţii
în vale opaiţul buturugilor putrede
însoţeşte mult timp.

MOULDING

It could be that I was a Celt
and that once upon a time I rooted about to rediscover the red heartstone
      of the mountains
in portfolios of flowers, dividing up with minute care
the fallen galleries,
the wide smile of the river
like a razor blade cutting the Valley of the Anie,
the Cormaia and the Ilves

could be that trick of spirits
and honeydew curdled in jerry cans
discoloured my hair
bleached my lashes and skin
      like a mosaic

that it numbed my powerless arms
helped by the vines surging along the beams

could be that distances
cut me down like millstones
in the shrivelled voice-box of a mill-race
between wooden wheels eroded
by brass, sand and carded wool

gold and lead
packs of wolves coming down more and more often
could be
and wild boars grunting close to the terraces
in the thick mist of the steepest slope
of mornings divided between unremitting tests

it could be that I was a Celt
my wide cheekbones superimposing themselves on other cheekbones:
in the valley the light from buried roots
stays with us a long time.

IATĂ-MĂ

Cîte simțăminte sînt eu
cum mă reazem de pocnetul de grisină al fiecărui fluture
căutînd să întrezăresc
    pielea pudrată a pomilor
    grădina casei de coji ronțăite
    iepurii molfăind iarna-n hăinuțe pufoase
    unii pe alții lepădîndu-se sub
    mereu scînteiosul briceag

cît de străină-mi sînt eu aici
într-o depărtare în care ceva ar putea să înceapă
și orice altceva s-ar putea vesteji
precum mălaiul în ceaunul bolborositor
precum nuferii mămăligii într-o fotografie
în care urmele mele sînt pulberea făcălețelor
scîncetul bătătoarelor pe care de uscăciune
aluatul a plesnit în altfel de hărți
    încetul cu încetul împreunîndu-și mînuțele
    năruindu-și făinoasele rotule
    pe țărîna în care zi și noapte-i totuna
o rugă înmiită pentru aducerile aminte
cu umbre de nuci înșurubate-n țeastă
    pe țărîna din noduri asfaltate
        atunci și acum
    pe țărîna
           corturi fluturătoare între degetele piciorului
           muruire desculță, gîngănii

ce oraș de mărunțișuri și scame am ajuns
ce trotuare cu obraji vineții de reziduuri
    cît de inerte băltuțele hăpăind cerul
        cu aeroplane cu tot
    și orizontul din creioane tocite

ce întindere necurmată de chipuri blonzii
hăhăind unele în cojile celorlalte
cînd timp doar ultimului i-a mai rămas

THAT'S ME

How many feelings I am
when I count on the crackle of a breadstick, of each butterfly
and when I try to glimpse
      the powdered skin of trees
      the heart of the house with ruined plaster
      rabbits munching on winter in their silky clothes
      all of them abandoning themselves to
      the ever-glistening pocket-knife

how strange I feel to myself
here in this distance where something could start
never mind what else may fade
like maize flour in the boiling pot
like water-lilies of polenta in a photograph,
where my tracks are the powder of rollers,
the whining of beaters so dried-out they've made
the dough crack up in other moulds
      little by little, putting their little hands together,
      their floury knees collapsing
      onto the earth where day and night are one
the prayer to remember them said a thousand times,
shadows of walnut-trees fixed in the head
      on the earth knots of asphalt
         in the beginning and now
      on the earth
            awnings undulating between the toes
            a barefoot rough-plastering, insects,

what town of jokes and floss have I come to
what pavements with cheeks blue with residues
      how motionless they are, the little pools which catch the sky
         including the aeroplanes
      and a horizon made by blunt crayons,

what an expanse interrupted by pale laughing faces
each in the skin of the last
till there's only one left

ce podiş străbătut de feţe nevrotice
şi ce chiuvete lipite cu leucoplast
în încuviinţările de pe vremea începutului
cînd palmele lor aspre îmi dezghiocau lacrimile
pe vînătăile cusute ale unui chip care
la fel de bine ar fi putut să nu fie

şi cum rătăcesc aidoma măturătorului
pe marginea beznei migălos îmbumbată
       către foirile dimineţii

şi cum mă acopăr cu propriile mîini
în încăperile de-atîtea ori nezugrăvite
şi cum mă bîlbîi ca un actoraş bun de nimic
spre nimicul ce din nimic se întremează
tricotîndu-şi tot mai încoace ecoul
       firul care ne leagă de ceea ce fi-va atunci
       oftatul care spre marginea filei aceleia
       ne va mai purta o vreme
       nişte invalizi
       cu stele strînse-n smocuri printre buchetele de coaste
       cu luna ciopîrţită în sfieli de rouă

şi cum mai tîndălesc ca un copil cretin
prostul satului pe toţi arătîndu-i cu degetul
ochi lunecoşi rostogolindu-se-n mingiuţe de ceară
şi broderii de pietre nemairăsuflînd
de încordare

iată-mă, iată
cu tot ce să fiu poate n-am apucat
deşi doar ce ţi se cuvine-n tăcere
cu asupra de măsură îţi este de-ajuns.

what a stage criss-crossed by neurotics
and what washbasins gummed up with sticking-plaster
in the compromises of early days
when their rough palms held my tears
against the stitched-up bruises of a face which
might as well not have existed

and how lost I am, like the street-sweeper
on the threshold between buttoned-down shadows
     and swarming morning

and how I hide myself with my own hands
in rooms whose walls are always unpainted
and how I stammer like a worthless little actor
about the nothingness which enlivens nothing
always knitting its echo closer
     the thread which ties us and which will therefore be
     the breath which will carry us one more time
     towards the border of this page,
     some of us injured,
     with the gathered-up stars in bunches among bouquets of flanks
     with the moon slashed by pink embarrassments

and how I dawdle like a stupid child
the village loony giving everyone the finger
petulant eyes rolling in little balls of wax
and decorations of stones no longer breathing
stiffened

that's me, there
with everything I probably haven't started to be yet
except what you're owed in silence
is immeasurably enough.

ACUM

De multe luni stau singură
şi dimineaţa ca un val de puroi
cu pomeţii a răzuit garsoniera

înainte în palma-mi Florin s-a uitat
         linia norocului nici nu există
(Mircea îmi spusese şi el)
         şi voi muri foarte tînără
mai tînără decît aş fi ştiut
decît totuşi aş fi înţeles

şi mi-e frică de moarte
mi-e frică s-o aştept ştiind că e
scheletul funinginii pe care
zi de zi îl respir

mi-e frică să rătăcesc
în mulţimea nopţilor identice
în duhoarea subsuorilor lor
mişunînd de vietăţi transparente

am fost măritată
nu am copii
femeile îndepărtate cu o lamă se şterg
şi am zăcut
amintindu-mi primii ani de facultate
nervii mei mereu la pămînt
nevoia de dragoste

am fost o fată
mai sînt o tînără fată
nici un impas în zestrea
acestor zgomote

e o sîmbătă
smulsă din torturantele pagini
dimineaţa mahmură a aţipit
pe geamurile garsonierei cu chirie

de fapt
         nicicînd nu mă voi întoarce...

NOW

I'm often alone
and morning, that wave of pus,
has scraped the studio from its cheekbones

earlier, Florin read in the lines of my hand
      that the line of fate hardly exists
(Mircea had already told me this, too)
      and I'll die very young
too young to know or understand
what's happening to me

and I'm afraid of death
I'm afraid to wait for it, knowing it's
the skeleton of soot which
I breathe daily

I'm afraid of getting lost
in the fog of identical nights
in the musty smell of their armpits
where transparent creatures swarm

I've been married
I don't have children
– women scarred with a blade obliterate themselves –
and lying down
I remembered the first years of freedom
when I lived always on my nerves
needing love,

I've been a girl
I'm still a young girl,
no let-up in this dowry
of sounds

it's a Saturday
snatched from the insufferable
the muddy morning drowsing
against the windows of the rented studio

so then
            I'll never come back…

Translated by Fiona Sampson

BULGARIA

PHOTO: TZVETELINA NIKOLAEVA

GEORGI GOSPODINOV was born in 1968 and writes poetry and fiction. His first two books, *Lapidarium* (1992) and *The Cherry-Tree of One People* (1996) – both poetry collections – immediately won him critical acclaim as well as a number of literary awards, and his debut novel, *Natural Novel* (1999) also received a national literary award and was later published in France, Serbia, and Macedonia. He brought out a collection of short stories in 2001 but his latest book, *Letters to Gaustin* (2003), is again a collection of poetry.

Gospodinov's poems and short stories have been published in periodicals in the USA, Germany, France, Hungary, Finland, Greece, and have also appeared in a number of anthologies of Bulgarian writing.

GEORGI GOSPODINOV

ЛЮБОВНИЯТ ЗАЕК

Ще се върна след малко, каза,
и остави вратата отворена.
Вечерта беше специална за нас,
върху печката къкреше заек,
беше нарязала лук, кръгчета моркови
и скилидки чесън.
Не си взе връхната дреха,
не сложи червило, не питах
къде отива.
Тя е такава.
Никога не е имала точна представа
за времето, закъснява за срещи, просто
така каза онази вечер –
Ще се върна след малко,
и дори не затвори вратата.

Шест години след тази вечер
я срещам на друга улица,
и ми се струва уплашена,
като някой, който се сеща,
че е забравил ютията включена
или нещо такова…

Изключи ли печката, пита тя.
Още не съм, казвам,

тези зайци са доста жилави.

THE LOVE RABBIT

I won't be long, she said
and left the door ajar.
It was a special evening for us,
a rabbit stew was slowly cooking on the hob,
she'd chopped some onions and garlic
and carrots into little disks.
She didn't take a coat
and didn't put on any lipstick; I didn't ask
where she was going.
She's like that.
She's never had any sense of time,
she's always late, that's all
she said that evening:
I won't be long;
she didn't even close the door.

Six years later
I meet her in the street (not our street)
and she suddenly seems worried
like someone who remembers
she forgot to unplug the iron
or something…

Did you turn the cooker off, she asks.
Not yet, I answer,

these rabbits can be very tough.

Translated by Kalina Filipova

ТАЙНИТЕ ВЕЧЕРИ НА ЕЗИКА

Обичам вечер порция език
от безсловесните
от онзи мускулест и жилав
език на крава вол или теле
език на немите
език на тези преди нас
език на дядо Уитман и на дядо ми
език на който псуваше
овцете с нега
език на който те разбраха
език на татко Елиът и на баща ми
познанството им твърде бегло
език на баба Емили на баба Лиза
и на баба ми когато мами
пчелата-майка с роя
мааать-mat-мааать*
език свещен
(ако пчелата не пристига
езикът стига)

Копнея тоз език езикът въобще
и съм признателен и никак
аз не съм гнуслив не се отвръщам
продължавам ви
ям пия раждам ви
тъй както само верни синове
дедите си изяждат пият
…

така навярно се постига
езикът всяка вечер

* така по нашия край мамят пчелите

THE LAST SUPPERS OF THE TONGUE

I like a piece of tongue for supper
of the speechless kind
muscular and tough
tongue of cow bull or calf
dumb tongue
tongue of our predecessors
tongue of grandpa Whitman and my grandpa
the tongue in which he cursed
the sheep with kindness
the tongue in which they understood
tongue of father Eliot and my own father
their acquaintance all too brief
tongue of grandma Emily and grandma Lisa
of my own grandma when she lures
the queen-bee and the swarm
maaat-mat-maaat*
the sacred tongue
(*the tongue alone will do*
if bees are few)

I long for such a tongue the tongue in general
and I am grateful and I'm not too
squeamish or repulsed
I keep on
eating drinking resurrecting you
just like the faithful sons
their fathers eat and drink
…

like this you probably attain
the tongue with every dish

Translated by Dimiter Kenarov

* That's how the bees are lured in our part of the country

GIRL

Кой ще чуе моя разказ за това момиче

Полягаш до момичето което
е лягало с момчето си което
е лягало с момичето което
е лягало с момчето си което
е лягало с момичето което

Полягаш приобщаваш се към всички

Виж цялата вселена е в леглото ти
Ах колко общество в едно момиче

ЙОАН

Нагазил до кръста в реката любовна
посрещам изпращам
посрещам изпращам
Ти ли си тази
Ти ли си тази
Ти ли си тази
дето има да идва

Или друга да чакам

GIRL

Is there anybody going to listen to my story

You lay the girl
who's laid the boy
who's laid his girl
who's laid the boy
who's laid his girl

You get laid you communicate

Look! the whole world's on your mattress
So much society in just one girl.

ST. JOHN

Wading up to my waist in the river of love
I receive and send off
Receive and send off
Are you the woman
Are you the woman
Are you the woman
that has to come

Or shall I wait for another.

Translated by Dimiter Kenarov

PHOTO: GEORGI GOSPODINOV

Nadezhda Radulova was born in 1975, graduated from the Bulgarian and English Departments at the University of Sofia in 1999 and went on to do an MPhil at the Central European University in Budapest and the Open University in London.

Her first book of poems, *A Name Struck Dumb*, was published in 1997 as a result of a competition organised by *Literaturen vestnik* and the publishing house Litse. In 2000 she published her second book of poems *Albas* with the publishers Janet-45.

In 2001 Nadezhda Radulova won the national Ivan Nikolov Young Author of the Year competition and in 2002 and 2003, took part in the Performing Literature Festival organized in Sofia by the British Council.

Radulova's poems have appeared in most of the important Bulgarian literary journals and weeklies, as well as on the internet. Some of her works are translated into English and Czech.

NADEZHDA RADULOVA

VICTORIA INN

треторазреден хотел на белгрейв роуд
от грамофона с фуния излиза кралица виктория
с рокля за първо причастие

отразена в стенното зацапано огледало
хотелиерката свежда очи
кашмирено сини очи под синята лампа
после дава въженце за скачане на виктория
и посяга към ключа за нашата стая

всяка вечер от година насам
трийсет и осем паунда включва все същото
изглед към задния двор
скъпо платени стенания от горните стаи
на закуска мюсли и сливово сладко
смяна на чаршафите сутрин
ала все същите нокти все същата кръв по чаршафите

ако някога просто се върнем случайно по пладне
ще видим виктория
по неглиже и състарена
възнак на софата слуша
грамофонната музика да излиза
този път някак хрипливо и на туберкули от
същата онази фуния

в тези редки случаи ти затваряш очите ми
и полека ме сваляш по стълбите към нашата стая
после ме слагаш да легна на студеното двойно легло
и целуваш ръцете ми
морави китки които някога някой връзвал е
сякаш с въженце за скачане

VICTORIA INN

a third rate hotel in the belgrave road
out of the horn of the gramophone queen victoria
emerges in her confirmation dress

reflected in the murky mirror on the wall
the hotel manager lowers her eyes
cashmere blue eyes under the blue lamp
then she hands victoria a skipping rope
and reaches for the key to our room

for years now every evening
thirty eight pounds sterling
for a view of the back yard
highly paid moans from the floor above
muesli and plum jam for breakfast
and a change of sheets in the morning
but it's always the same nails and the same blood on them

if we ever happen to come back around noon
we'll see victoria
dishevelled and looking old
stretched out on the sofa
listening to music coming
hoarsely this time and in tubercules
out of the same gramophone horn

on those rare occasions you close my eyes
and slowly take me down to our room
then you lay me down upon the cold double bed
and kiss my hands
the purple wrists which someone once tied
with what might have been a skipping rope

ПЛОДОВА ДИЕТА

докосвам те околоплодно
около шест и десет сутрин
около третия етаж
около сто и трийстия сонет на шекспир
стомахът е паница с похлупак
четиринайсет стъпала нагоре
околошекспир
околосонет
околоплодно те докосвам
най-първо кожицата свличам
и в нервната си рокля те обличам
обичам в най-изгнилия участък
самичка да изсмуча сладостта
като пчела до сълзи да залепна
за дръжката а след това
със зъби я изтеглям в шест и двайсет
спасително въже отвътре
изригва риган бял равнец и бучиниш
букет за мургавата господарка
от сто и трийстия сонет
коя е тя коя съм аз
гладът е скучно цвете за глупачки

изпичам ябълката в мед до зачервяване
полекичка събувам си сандалите

ТРЕВИ ЗА ЛЕТЕНЕ

устата ти е евтина гондола
венеция е някъде навътре
ала наместо тициан и каса д'оро
прелитам през дворци от зъбен камък

по улици от шестнадесетини
лъкът ми се обтяга и разпуска
додето се успокоят стрелите
в базиликата на безкрайните ти пръсти

FRUIT DIET

aboutfruitfully I touch you
about ten past six in the morning
about the third floor
about shakespeare's sonnet 130
the stomach is a lidded bowl
up fourteen steps
aboutshakespeare
aboutsonnets
aboutfruitfully I touch you
first I peel off the skin
and dress you in my nervy dress
I like to suck the sweetness out myself
out of the most rotten part
to stick like a bee
to the stem and then
at six-twenty pull out with my teeth
a life-saving rope from the inside
milfoil marjoram hemlock erupt
a posy for the dark lady
of sonnet 130
who is she who am I
hunger is a boring flower for silly women

I bake the apple dipped in honey till it's browned
and gently slip off my sandals

GRASS FLIGHTS

my mouth is a cheap gondola
venice is somewhere deep inside
but instead of titian and casa d'oro
I fly through palaces of kidney stones

along semiquaver streets
my bow tautens and slackens
until the arrows calm down
in the basilica of your elongated fingers

и ето акватичното ти тяло
обагря се във витаминен климат
надолу още по-надолу
ме потопяват няколко амфибии

релефът тука е съвсем различен
ръцете ми се взират без да дишам
Вечният Град навярно всеки миг
пред устните ми ще изплува

като риба

ЕДИСОН

досущ котка захапала малкото за вратлето
светлината ме влачи из цялата стая
докато жили издуят стените
и килимът изплюе своето вълнено синьо сърце
в къщата няма стопани
само желания:

да се измъкна от пола си
от лявата си половина
от последната си твърдина литературата

котката е къпина която гори в средата на стаята
там се сбъдват всички желания
без умора
и без да оставят ненужни следи

после котката спи под кревата
после отново танцуваме
сипвам мляко в паничката
даже млякото свети

за приятелка имам махарани от далечна страна

and there your aquatic body
is tanning in a vitamin climate
I'm sunk deeper and deeper
by several amphibians

the terrain is very different here
my hands are peering around I'm not breathing
any moment now the Eternal City
will probably swim by before my lips

like a fish

EDISON

just like a cat carrying her kitten by the scruff of the neck
the light drags me about the room
until the veins bulge inside the walls
and the carpet spits out its blue woollen heart

no hosts in the house
only wishes:

to slip out of my sex
out of my left side
out of my last fortress literature

the cat is a blackberry bush burning in the middle of the room
that's where every wish comes true
tirelessly
and without leaving any needless trace

then the cat sleeps under the bed
then we dance again
I pour milk in the bowl
even the milk glows

my friend is a maharani from a distant country

АЛБА ЗА ЛЕКОТО ХРАНЕНЕ

ти питаш ме какво сънувам нощем:

сънят ми винаги е без пижама
цял мускули и мускус муселин
са пръстите му кирие елейсон
са пръстите му есенни съпруже

додето си лежиш тежат в стомаха ти
змиорките като смарагди
се дави ноемврийската оса
тъй шумно в снощното бургундско
уж малко грахчето било ала
е твърде нежен хълбока ти принце

а можехме да поиграем инак:

да изберем глада
телата да постелим
прозрачни като брюкселски чаршафи
и с пръсти да си подредим словата
в салати здравословни
и две-три капки течен мед
в млечния път да впръскаме
за сън
а и за вкус

сега наместо муселин и мед
лъжичка мента
ще разреди гастритната ти горест
но само спри да бърчиш нос
невчесан влажен пудел

сутрин
мириша на това
което съм сънувала последно

ALBA TO LIGHT MEALS

you ask me what I dream at night:

my dream is always naked no pyjamas
all muscles musk and muslin
are its fingers *kyrie eleison*
are its fingers my autumn husband

and while you're lying there in your stomach
the eels are heavy like emeralds
and the november wasp is drowning
so noisily in last night's burgundy
supposedly the pea was small
but your flank is sensitive my prince

and yet we could have played a different game:

we could have chosen hunger
spread out our bodies
diaphanous like sheets of needle lace
and with our fingers we could have
arranged our words in healthy salads
a drop or two of liquid honey
we could have poured into the milky way
for sleep
or for flavour

but now instead of milk and muslin
we add a hint of mint
to water down your gastric grief
but don't keep puckering your nose
you damp dishevelled poodle

mornings
I smell of whatever
I dreamt last night

Translated by Kalina Philipova

ESTONIA

RICHARD ADANG was born in 1953 in New York, grew up in several US states as well as in Germany and Greece and graduated from Indiana University in 1977 with a BA in English and Psychology. Since coming to Estonia in 1995, he has been an English teacher at Rapla Co-Educational High School and has had poems published in several American journals including *Harper's* and *The Paris Review* and the Estonian journal *Looming*. He has translated the work of a number of Estonian poets and his first book, *The Light In Estonia* (bilingual), was published in 2001.

TAAVI TATSI was born in 1978 and is a freelance translator and lecturer at Viljandi Cultural Academy. He studied history and philosophy at Tartu University and at Valdosta State University in the USA. He is one of the translators of Robert Bly's *Iron John* into Estonian and has contributed to translations into English of poems by Kristiina Ehin and Andres Ehin.

ERIC DICKENS was born in 1953 and studied at the University of East Anglia. His translations of the works of the Estonian writers Jan Kross, Arvo Valton and Rein Tootmaa have been published in book form in the UK by, among others, Harvill, Picador and Index on Censorship. He also translates from, and into, Dutch and Swedish.

LATVIA

HÅKAN BRAVINGER, a Swedish poet and translator, is employed by the Swedish Writers Union and is currently working on his second book of poetry. His translation of Timofeyev's 'Resistance with Mickey Mouse' (pp. 62-67) was originally made for the Stockholm Poetry Festival in 2000.

RIHARDS KALNIŅŠ studied audio-visual culture and philosophy before starting to work as a translator. He has translated numerous humanitarian articles, literary criticism and the work of several young Latvian poets.

IEVA LEŠINSKA is a writer and translator living and working in Riga. Her translations of Latvian poetry regularly appear in both Latvian and foreign publications and she has published a number of translations of Anglo-American poetry into Latvian, including T. S. Eliot's *The Waste Land*, Allen Ginsberg's *Kaddish*, as well as selected poems by Robert Frost, Seamus Heaney, Ted Hughes, D. H. Lawrence, Ezra Pound, Dylan Thomas and others. Her original poetry has appeared in Latvian periodicals and anthologies and she is currently writing a book of 'documentary fiction'.

IRINA OSADCHAJA is a journalist and translator from Riga with a particular interest in rock-poetry, as a result of which she has translated the lyrics of a number of Latvian rock groups into English. She worked on the translation of Timofeyev's 'A man comes in…' (p. 59) with the American language poet Lyn Hejinian.

LITHUANIA

EUGENIJUS ALIŠANKA was born in 1960 and for ten years, until 2000, worked as a scientific researcher at the Institute of Culture and Art in Vilnius. In 1994, he became a director of the international programmes – and also a member of the Board – at the Lithuanian Writers' Union, and since 2003 has been Editor-in-chief of the Union's magazine, *The Vilnius Review*. A member of Lithuanian PEN and executive director of the international poetry festival 'Poetry Spring', he is a poet and essayist with a number of published collections to his name, as well as being a well-known translator.

KERRY SHAWN KEYS was born in Pennsylvania in the USA and now lives in Vilnius where he currently works freelance as a poet, translator and in cultural liaison. He has over forty books to his credit which include translations from Portuguese, Czech and Lithuanian, and his own poems, rooted in the Appalachia hill country and in Brazil and India where he lived for a considerable time. In 1992, he received the Robert H. Winner Memorial Award from the Poetry Society of America. Selected poems have appeared in Czech and Lithuanian.

JONAS ZDANYS was born in the United States to Lithuanian parents in 1950 and still lives and works there. He is a graduate of Yale University, with a PhD from the State University of New York. He is author of 29 books, 26 of which are collections of his own poetry written in English and in Lithuanian, and of his translations of Lithuanian poetry and prose into English. He has received a number of prestigious literary awards for his own poetry and for his translations.

POLAND

ANTONIA LLOYD-JONES is a full-time translator of Polish literature whose published work includes fiction by Jaroslaw Iwaszkiewicz, Olga Tokarczuk and Pawel Huelle. She also translates non-fiction, most recently Joanna Olczak-Ronikier's biography of her Polish-Jewish family, *In the Garden of Memory*.

W. MARTIN edited a special Polish literature issue of *Chicago Review* in 2000. His published translations include Natasza Goerke's *Farewells to Plasma* (Twisted Spoon Press, 2001) and Heinrich von Kleist's 'Friedrich's Seascape' in the magazine *Parakeet* (2004).

CZECH REPUBLIC

ALEXANDRA BÜCHLER was born in Prague and has lived in Greece, Australia and Great Britain. A translator of fiction, poetry, theatre plays and texts on modern art and architecture, she has over twenty-five books to her name, including six anthologies of contemporary Czech, Australian, Scottish and Greek short stories.

JUSTIN QUINN was born in Dublin, educated at Trinity College, Dublin and since 1995 has taught at Charles University in Prague. He has published three collections of poetry (the first of which, *The O'o'a'a' Bird* (1994), was short-listed for the Forward Prize) and also a critical study of Wallace Stevens. He has written extensively on modern American poetry, and is a co-editor of the Irish poetry magazine *Metre*.

SLOVAKIA

JAMES SUTHERLAND-SMITH is a poet and a leading translator of Slovak poetry into English, responsible for the first anthology of contemporary Slovak poetry translated into English, *Not Waiting For Miracles* in 1993. He also translated the anthology *One Hundred Years of Slovak Literature*, edited by Stanislava Repar and published in 2000, into English. With his wife Viera, James has translated the selected poems of a number of individual Slovak poets including Ján Búzassy, Mila Haugová, Ivan Laučík, Jozef Leikert and Milan Rúfus. He is currently Project Manager for the Peacekeeping English Project advising the Armed Forces of Serbia and Montenegro. James's most recent collection of his own work is *In the Country of the Birds* (Carcanet, 2003), his previous book of poems being *At the Skin Resort* published by Arc in 1999.

KATERINA SUTHERLAND-SMITHOVÁ was born in 1985 and is James Sutherland-Smith's daughter. Currently completing her gymanzium education in Prešov, she hope to study Law. She is fluent in Slovak, Czech, English and German and sings jazz with local bands in Slovakia.

MARTIN SOLOTRUK is a poet with two published collections to his name, and is also a well-known translator, his translations of, among others, Ted Hughes, John Ashbery, Seamus Heaney and Charles Simic having appeared in book form and in magazines in Slovakia. He currenntly teaches at the Comenius University in Bratislava.

SLOVENIA

ANA JELNIKAR, a native of Ljubljana, received her secondary school education in London and graduated in English and Sociology from the University of Ljubljana. She teaches English and translates extensively both into Slovenian and English. Her translations have been published in such literary magazines as *Verse, Southern Humanities Review, Third Coast,* and *The American Poetry Review.* She is also the translator of the first Slovenian edition of C. G. Jung's *Man and His Symbols.*

HUNGARY

MICHAEL CASTRO is an American poet and university professor, living and working in St. Louis, Missouri. He has published seven books of poetry and a book of essays entitled *Interpreting the Indian: 20th Century Poets and the Native American* (University of Oklahoma Press, 1992).

GÁBOR G. GYUKICS was born in Budapest in 1958 but has lived in the United States since 1988. A poet and literary translator, he is an associate member of the Academy of American Poets and his work has appeared in several magazines and anthologies in the USA, Japan and Europe. He has published three collections of poetry and two volumes of translations.

DAVID HILL is a poet and performance artist whose work has appeared in films, on pop records, at festivals, in anthologies published on four continents, and in a wide range of literary magazines. He has published two collections, *Angels and Astronauts* and *Bald Ambition.* He lives in Budapest, where he co-runs The Bardroom, an English-language show featuring poetry, music and the spoken word by local and visiting performers.

PETER SHERWOOD has taught at the School of Slavonic and East European Studies, University of London, and his most recent publication is *The Oxford Learners English-Hungarian Dictionary* (OUP, 2002).

GEORGE SZIRTES was born in Budapest in 1948 and came to England as a refugee, following the Hungarian Uprising in 1956. His family settled in London and he trained as a painter in Leeds and London. He has published thirteen collections of poetry from *The Slant Door* (Secker, 1979) to *An English Apocalypse* (Bloodaxe, 2001). His *Selected Poems* were published by Oxford University Press in 1996. He has also produced many works of translation, books for children and a study of the artist Ana Maria Pacheco.

ROMANIA

FIONA SAMPSON is a poet and translator with many published books to her name, among the most recent being *Travel Diary* (Knixebna Akademija, Macdonia, 2004), *Creative Writing in Health and Social Care* (Jessica Kingsley, 2004) and *Evening Brings Everything Back* (translations of Jaan Kaplinski, Bloodaxe, 2004). She has also written for radio and public art commission and has been published and broadcast in many European countries. She is AHRB Research Fellow in the Creative and Performing Arts at Oxford Brookes University's Centre for Modern and Contemporary Poetry, Editor of *Orient Express* and, in the USA, of *Context*.

ADAM J. SORKIN has published sixteen books of translation and numerous poets and poems in literary journals. His translation of prose poems by Ioana Ieronim, *The Triumph of the Water Witch,* (Bloodaxe, 2000) was short-listed for the Weidenfeld Prize and three of his translations have been nominated for Pushcart Prize volumes. His collaborative translations have appeared in more than 225 literary magazines including *The New Yorker* and *American Poetry Review.*

BULGARIA

KALINA FILIPOVA graduated in English Language and Literature at Sofia University and currently teaches there. She translates poetry and fiction from, and into, Bulgarian and English and her work is included in a number of English- language anthologies of Bulgarian poetry. Her most recent translations are included in *Performing Literature: British and Bulgarian Authors in Sofia*, published by the British Council in Sofia.

DIMITER KENAROV holds a BA degree in American and Russian Literature from Middleburry College, Boston, Massachusetts. He translates contemporary American poetry into Bulgarian and is author of a poetry book in Bulgarian published in 2001.

Jean Boase-Beier is Senior Lecturer in Translation Studies, Linguistics and German at the University of East Anglia, where she runs the MA in Literary Translation. She has translated poetry by Volker von Törne, Rose Ausländer (*Mother Tongue*, translated with Anthony Vivis, published by Arc Publications in 1995) and is Editor of Arc's 'Visible Poets' series. She has written extensively on translation, especially the translation of poetry. Her most recent books are: (ed., with Michael Holman) *The Practices of Literary Translation: Constraints and Creativity*, published in 1999 by St Jerome Press; (with Ken Lodge) *The German Language*, published by Blackwell in 2003; and a translation of Ernst Meister's selected poems published under the title *Between Nothing and Nothing* in Arc Publications' 'Visible Poets' series, also in 2003.

Alexandra Büchler was born in Prague and has lived in Greece, Australia and Great Britain. She is Director of Literature Across Frontiers, a programme of international literary exchange and policy debate, based in Wales, and member of the editorial board of the European Internet Review of Books and Writing, *Transcript*. A translator of fiction, poetry, theatre plays and texts on modern art and architecture, she has translated over twenty-five books, including six anthologies of contemporary Czech, Australian, Scottish and Greek short stories. Among the many authors she has translated are J. M. Coetzee, David Malouf, Jean Rhys, Janice Galloway and Rhea Galanaki.

Fiona Sampson is a poet and editor. Her most recent books are: *Patuvacki Dnevnik* ('Travel Diary'), (Knixevna Akademija, Macedonia, 2004); *Creative Writing in Health and Social Care* (Jessica Kingsley, 2004); *Evening Brings Everything Back* (translations of Jaan Kaplinski, Bloodaxe, 2004); *Folding the Real* (Seren, 2001); *The Healing Word* (The Poetry Society, 1999); *The Self on the Page* (with Celia Hunt, Jessica Kingsley, 1998 and published in Hebrew by Ach, 2002); and, forthcoming, *Creative Writing and the Writer* (with Celia Hunt, Palgrave-Macmillan 2005) and volumes in Serbian and Romanian.

She has also written for radio and public art commission. She has been published and broadcast in Polish, Serbian, Hebrew, Romanian, Finnish, Norwegian, Catalan, Bulgarian, Slovakian, Slovenian and Macedonian. Awards include the 2003 Zlaten Prsten for international writing (Macedonian Foundation for Culture and Sciences), a Hawthornden Fellowship, the Newdigate Prize; and awards from the Arts Councils of England and Wales and the Society of Authors. Fiona Sampson is AHRB Research Fellow in the Creative and Performing Arts at Oxford Brookes University's Centre for Modern and Contemporary Poetry; and Editor of *Orient Express*, a journal of contemporary writing from Enlargement Europe and, in the USA, of *Context*.

Other titles in Arc Publications'
Translation Series include:

ROSE AUSLÄNDER
(Germany)
Mother Tongue: Selected Poems
TRANSLATED BY JEAN BOASE-BEIER & ANTHONY VIVIS

CEVAT ÇAPAN
(Turkey)
Where Are You, Susie Petschek?
TRANSLATED BY CEVAT ÇAPAN & MICHAEL HULSE
INTRODUCTION BY A. S. BYATT
'Visible Poets' translation series No. 6 (parallel-text)

JEAN CASSOU
(France)
33 Sonnets of the Resistance
TRANSLATED BY TIMOTHY ADÈS
INTRODUCTION BY ALISTAIR ELLIOT
'Visible Poets' translation series No. 7 (parallel-text)

BARTOLO CATTAFI
(Italy)
Anthracite
TRANSLATED BY BRIAN COLE
INTRODUCTION BY PETER DALE
'Visible Poets' translation series No. 1 (parallel-text)

CLAUDE DE BURINE
(France)
Words Have Frozen Over
TRANSLATED BY MARTIN SORRELL
INTRODUCTION BY SUSAN WICKS
'Visible Poets' translation series No. 5 (parallel-text)

ARJEN DUINKER
(Holland)
The Sublime Song of a Maybe
TRANSLATED BY WILLIAM GROENEWEGEN
INTRODUCTION BY JEFFREY WAINWRIGHT
'Visible Poets' translation series No. 8 (parallel-text)

GABRIEL FERRATER
(Catalonia)
Women and Days
TRANSLATED BY ARTHUR TERRY
INTRODUCTION BY SEAMUS HEANEY
'Visible Poets' translation series No. 13 (parallel-text)